W9-BWP-706

Attention: Teachers/Supervisors/Administrators

MATH WORKSHOPS

Teacher/Student Workshops ▲ Family Math Night ▲ Staff Development

MATH IN MOTION: ORIGAMI IN YOUR CLASSROOM

where every child counts...

What is the Math in Motion (MIM) Program?

Math in Motion is a HANDS-ON, interdisciplinary and creative approach to teaching mathematics using origami. Workshops are designed to explore the applications of paper folding to shape and size recognition, spatial sense, patterns, geometry, listening to and following directions, making connections, interpreting diagrams, sequencing, critical thinking and problem solving...

Learn how to bring out the BEST ☆ in even *your* most reluctant, "I hate math,"ESL or gifted.

What is the Goal of MIM Workshops?

1) Make Math ғυℕ 2) Support Nat'l Math Standards 3) Teach Cultural Diversity
ALL children develop math pΘwer and discover the beauty, symmetry, precision, mystery, excitement and joy of mathematics!

Who Should Participate?

All Grade ∅ (K-6) Teachers and Students, Teachers of ESL/LEP, Title l/Chapter l, Gifted, Resource Specialist, At-Risk, Special Education, Student Teachers, Curriculum Coordinators, Supervisors, Mentors, Parents and Aides.

Some Sponsors of the Math in Motion Program

National Council of Teachers of Mathematics (NCTM)
California Association for the Gifted (CAG)
Association of Mathematics Teachers of New York (AMTNYS)
California Association for Bilingual Education (CABE)
San Antonio Independent Schools
National Montessori Center for Education
Association of Christian Schools International
National Council of Supervisors of Mathematics (NCSM)

"In her Math in Motion workshops and book, Barbara has created a wonderfully delightful and practical guide to using origami that makes math come alive in the hands and minds of all children." --Steven Leinwand, President, Nat'l Council of Supervisors of Mathematics

FOR MORE INFORMATION, CALL FASCINATING FOLDS:

☎ 1-800-968-2418
E-Mail: Pearl2@earthlink.net
Visit our Teacher's Corner WEB SITE: http://www.fascinating-folds.com/paper

Do your students come to school excited about mathematics?
Is math their favorite subject? This program will help you
make a difference! Build a brighter tomorrow with...

Math

Motion

Origami in the Classroom
A Hands-On Creative Approach
to Teaching Mathematics

In Appreciation...

Every book is the work of many hands and I gratefully acknowledge and appreciate the following people.

Helene Selig, my mother, for her joie de virve.

Jason Seth Houten, my son, for his creative imagination and illustrations.

Cathy Faith Janson, for her sense of humour and valuable ideas.

Carol LeKashman, architect and cherished friend, for her editing.

Maura McDonald, M.F.C.C., school counselor, for her heartfelt editing.

Faiga Rubinstein, M.D., for her assistance with the Spanish translation.

Lorne Houten, Ph.D., M.D., mathematician, for his technical advice.

Marylyn Rosenblum and Susan Johnson, Brøderbund Software, Inc., special thanks for all their generous time and cooperation.

Newport Beach Public Library Staff, for their reference.

Teachers, Students and Parents, for their participation and testing MIM.

Family and Friends, for their enthusiasm, encouragement and support.

Chelsea and Seven, for their canine and feline devotion and loyal vigil.

Acknowledgments...

ClickArt and T/Maker Company for their software graphics.

Cooking the Chinese Way. Fortune Cookies, by Ling Yu. ©1982 by Lerner Publications. Used by Permission of the publisher. All Rights Reserved.

Diagrams by John Jacecko, Quantum Labs, Corona del Mar, California.

Fun Folds, Language Learning through Paper Folding. Laura Grey and Rachel Katz. Tucson, Arizona: Communication Skill Builders, 1984.

Graphics reproduced using The Print Shop®; ©1985, 1984, Brøderbund Software, Inc. All Rights Reserved. Used by Permission.

Love Notes. Sandra Ramney. <u>Arithmetic Teacher</u>, September 1993, p 87.

Math Anxiety Cartoon and Japanese Fan by Lindsey and John Minko.

<u>New York Newsday</u>. "Discovery". Face Folding, Debra Soloman. 1992.

Origami Made Easy. The Power of Association, P. 15, by Kunihiko Kasahara. ©1973. Japan Publications, Inc. Used by Permission of the publisher. All Rights Reserved.

Origami USA. Jan Polish, Board of Directors.

The Magic of Origami. How to Make an Origami Mobile, P.79, by Alice Gray and Kunihiko Kasahara ©1977 by Japan Publications, Inc. Used by Permission of the publisher. All Rights Reserved.

"The journey of a thousand miles begins with a single step."
...Chinese proverb

"We make a living by what we get, but we make a life by what we give."
...Winston Churchill

"We have learned so much. I didn't know math could be this much fun!"
...An eleven year old girl after a workshop

To Parents and Educators:

" I think, at a child's birth, if a mother could ask a fairy godmother to
endow it with the most useful gift, that gift should be curiosity."

--*Eleanor Roosevelt (1983)*

This is not a book on teaching your child *how* to do math. Instead, it is a book on teaching your child to *want* to learn math. Jaime Escalante, a Bolivian immigrant and the celebrated math teacher portrayed in the film *Stand and Deliver*, turned an impoverished predominantly Hispanic East Los Angeles High School into a national math powerhouse. Escalante believed *ganas*, (desire), is one of the most important ingredients for learning. How does one begin to instill in children the desire to *want* to learn?

One of the primary learning methods for children is imitation. Children imitate what they hear and see. In the classroom children often hear and see negative messages about mathematics. They associate it with worksheets, textbooks, and tests. Many parents and teachers report they are uncomfortable teaching mathematics and may subconsciously transfer negative messages that influence their children's attitudes towards mathematics. As a national speaker, I meet hundreds of people every year who exclaim, "I hate math! I was never good at math! Math was my worse subject!" These messages perpetuate the cycle that math exclusively focuses on mind-numbing routines and mechanical and technical procedures. *Math in Motion* believes that math ability is related to *attitude* versus *aptitude* and that **ALL** children, especially girls, and minorities can develop MATH P☼WER!

Parent involvement leads to children's success and is one of the ways they can influence their children's development. I began reading aloud and playing math related games with my son, Jason from an early age...singing nursery rhymes and counting the stars in the galaxy. We collected magnets that framed our refrigerator door that we categorized, sorted and classified. At the supermarket, we weighed apples and estimated the price of potatoes. As Jason grew older, he developed a love for reading, mathematics, and learning. Once a week we visited the library, checked out our favorite books and attended special programs. One day, Michael Shall, the President of Origami USA was teaching an origami workshop at a Manhattan library in New York City. "Hands in lap before you start,"... we were captivated by the beauty, symmetry, and mystery of paperfolding.

Math in Motion invites you to discover the creative language of mathematics through *Origami in the Classroom*. I promise you that once you share some of these activities together, they will become one of the best parts of your day and you will treasure them for years to come. Whether you're a student teacher, a software programmer, an engineer or a mother raising a family, I hope that you will find some useful ideas in this book and unfold the joys and challenges of learning mathematics.

—*Barbara Erica Pearl*

Table of Contents

*Teacher Scripts

Part VI
Cultural & Educational Enrichment

Part VII
Resources

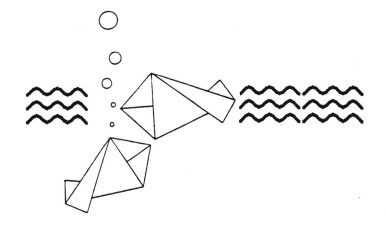

Make it Happen in Your Classroom
(Strategies for Getting Students Excited about Mathematics and Learning
(Stimulating Projects to Make your Math Program Soar
(Methods for Boosting your Students' Confidence
(Eliminate Fears of Failure

Building Math Literacy
⚮ Learn to Communicate Mathematically
⚮ Visualizing Math Concepts: Seeing is Believing
⚮ Non-threatening Ways to get Kids to Participate
⚮ Develop a Positive Math Environment for ALL Students

Skill Building Without Paper and Pencil
⚷ Organize your Classroom for Active Participation
⚷ Less Disruptive and More On-Task Behavior
⚷ Cooperative Learning Activities to Connect Math
⚷ Across the Curriculum

Teaching for Understanding
☆ Meaningful "Hands-On" Manipulatives for Developing
☆ Understanding and Spatial Sense
☆ Minds in Motion: Learning by Doing
☆ Proven, Practical, Easy Ideas to Integrate Curriculum
☆ Multicultural

"In her *Math in Motion* workshops and book, Barbara Pearl has created a wonderfully delightful and practical guide to using origami that makes mathematics come alive in the hands and minds of all children."
Steven Leinwand, President, National Council of Supervisors of Mathematics (NCSM)

"Many of my student teachers hate math and are scared of it. After one of them used *Math in Motion* to demonstrate a lesson, the class broke into spontaneous applause! Your method gave her the confidence to excel. I am convinced that your method is an invaluable tool for all grade levels."
Davida Fischman, Asst. Professor, California State San Bernardino

"Barbara is unparalleled in her ability to connect origami to math concepts and spatial skills. I use *Math in Motion* with my preservice and inservice teachers as well as children. They now respond to math with great anticipation and joy!"
Janet G. Melancon, Ed.D., Associate Professor, Loyola University New Orleans

"It was great! Lots of ideas and enthusiasm. Thanks for making our Staff Development Day so successful."
Sandra E. Barry, Assistant Superintendent

"*Math in Motion* is a hit! Highly motivating and inspirational. Count us in. Let's do it again."
Kathy Levenshus, PTA Council President

"*Math in Motion* is so easy to follow and makes learning math with my daughter fun!"
Denise DeLeon, Parent, 8th Grade

"Now millions of viewers have an opportunity to learn about this exciting and innovative method of teaching. I wish I had learned math this way when I was in school!"
Gary Collins, Home Show, ABC Television

"Excellent work with student assemblies, great crowd control–children were really excited! Math is everywhere!"
David Washington, Kindergarten

"Fascinating and dynamic presentation–the children were so attentive and responsive. Next year begins a new approach to math using manipulatives. *Math in Motion* will be a great addition! Come back soon!"
Carol Allen, 4th Grade, Outstanding Teacher of the Year

"Fabulous insights for my math program. *Math in Motion* makes my math classes come alive!"
Sheila Bloom, 5th grade, Chapter 1

"I thoroughly enjoyed your workshop. My students response to your program was overwhelming!!!"
Jeffrey Ballam, 6th grade, Gifted Education

"Great for relating math to art especially since I work with students who like to touch to learn! The visuals were an excellent way of introducing math vocabulary and concepts, especially for those who don't like math."
Maria Perez, 3rd Grade, Bilingual Education

What Children are Saying...

"Your teaching is so nice. I like the way you taught us. I wish I could be a teacher like you."
Joseph Walker, 2nd Grade

"Our whole class cherishes your teaching. Your classes are really fun! Can we do more of this?"
Minh Nguyen, 4th Grade

"I usually don't like math, but now I want to learn more. I'm glad we have your lessons and someone is here to help me. I just wish you could stay longer."
Nina Perez, 6th Grade

Photo: Patrick Janson, Amanda Hansen and Melanie Lee discover the excitement and joy of mathematics as they unfold a *Math in Motion* model of the origami box.

 hayo (greetings) and welcome...to an exciting educational program that makes every child count! *Math in Motion* (MIM), is a creative and interdisciplinary approach to teaching mathematics using origami, the art of Japanese paper folding.

 each inside to find a variety of materials for every grade level that will empower you and your students mathematically! One of the greatest values of MIM is the sense of accomplishment and achievement your students will experience as they gain a positive attitude towards math.

 invite you to explore ways to incorporate these pages into your lessons. MIM is based on the principle that children learn by doing, and supports the national goals for "hands-on" learning. Make math come alive!

 eometry, shape, number and pattern recognition, fractions, spatial sense, listening and following directions, comparing, communicating, graphing, investigating, problem solving, and analytical thinking are just some of the valuable skills MIM uses to develop meaning and understanding in math.

 ll children are captivated by the origami experience. MIM is committed to demystifying the fear and elitism often associated with math and invites children to feel, touch and *see the concepts* being taught. Children exclaim, "I did it! I didn't know math could be this much fun! Teach us more!"

 ath in Motion encourages recycling resources. Learn how to use a variety of budget friendly and recyclable materials from magazines to newspapers. MIM also promotes global education, an understanding and appreciation of differences by teaching tolerance for cultural diversity.

 f you would like to help your child excel in math and discover easy, practical ideas, that make learning $_F{_U}^N$...enter the fold!

Part I

Introduction
to
Math in Motion

*E*ducation is helping children realize their potential.

Erich Fromm

Introduction

**"I hear and I forget.
I see and I remember.
I do and I understand."**
...Chinese Proverb

Does YOUR head ☺ start to itch every time you have to solve a math problem? Does your vision 👀 get blurry when you try to balance your checkbook? Many of my students suffer from "M^A^T^H A_N_XI^E^T_Y." A page of numbers fills them with paniC! CBS columnist, Charles Osgood, states, "Some people have such an aversion to math when confronted with numbers or calculations their teeth start to ache!"

Math in Motion (MIM), is designed to relieve math anxiety and to draw kids into the world of learning. This hands-on "see-it, say-it, write-it" method helps you and your children enjoy and learn to communicate mathematically. It is easy to learn, simple to use, and a valuable teaching tool that creates an exciting dimension to your math learning environment. This successful program demonstrates proven, practical, and non-threatening ways to bring out the BEST ☆ in even *your* most reluctant... "I hate math," ESL or gifted students.

Paper folding invites children to explore geometric patterns and abstract concepts. Shapes ○ ❀ □ and forms take on a part of their mental image of the world in which they live and help to bridge that gap between words and their meaning. Through the paper folding process children feel successful and motivated to learn. Teachers discover special methods to focus attention, sharpen concentration, memory and recall. *Math in Motion* supports the national goals for teaching mathematics--to help **ALL** children develop MATH P○WER!

-13-

History of Origami

What is the history of origami?

Origami is a Japanese word for paperfolding. "Ori," the verb, means to fold. "Gami," (kami) the noun, means paper. Paper folding dates back over 1000 years ago to parts of Europe and China. Buddhist monks then carried paper from China by way of Korea into Japan. As paper was so precious and expen$ive, it was originally preserved by the religious leaders and emperors. For centuries, origami was associated with traditional Japanese ceremonies; however, over time, it became a family pastime and was handed down from one generation to the next.

Who were some famous paperfolders?

Leonardo da Vinci, (1452-1519), included a number of geometric paperfolding exercises in his study on the velocity and motion of paper. Other famous paper folders include: Lewis Carroll, (1832-1898), a mathematician and the author of *Alice in Wonderland;* Miguel de Unamuno, (1864-1936), a Spanish philosopher and poet; Friedrich Froebel, a famous German educator who founded the kindergarten system in the 1800's and used origami to familiarize children with geometric shapes; and Harry Houdini, a magician and the author of one of the first English origami books in 1922. Today there are active origami societies throughout the world that link cultures and nations together. An annual origami convention is held in New York City by Origami USA. Although origami attracts people from all over the world, many enthusiasts are mathematicians, scientists and engineers. Peter Engle, an architect, in *Folding the Universe* refers to origami as the, "mathematician's art."

Why is origami so special?

Origami is special because all you need is a piece (*peace*) of paper. (Throughout history the crane has been recognized as an international symbol of *peace.* According to Japanese legend if you fold a thousand cranes you will get your wish and live a long life. The legend of the crane is illustrated in Eleanor Coerr's children's story, *Sadako and the Thousand Paper Cranes*). Paperfolding also has many therapeutic benefits and is used in speech, mental health and occupational therapy. Seth, an enthusiastic fifth grader said, "It's like a journey inside the paper! My days can be hectic, but with origami I can put *everything* in order." Tomoko Fuse, a celebrated and prolific origami author, relates, "All origami begins with putting the hands into motion. Understanding something intellectually and knowing the same thing tactilely are very different."

Mathematics & Origami

"A mathematician, like a painter or poet, is a maker of patterns...with ideas."
—Godfrey H. Hardy (1877-1947)

A square is transformed into a box.
A square is transformed into a bird.
A square is transformed into a snake.
A square is transformed into an elephant.

Unless one knew better, one would think we were talking about a magic show or topology[1].

Origami is an art form that dates back to 583 A.D. when Buddhist monks brought paper into Japan from China through Korea. Since the manufacturing of paper at that time was costly, people used it with care, and origami became an integral part of certain ceremonies. The art of origami has been shared and passed on from generation to generation. Animals, flowers, boats, and people have all been created with origami. (The word origami is derived from *ori—to fold* and *gami—paper*.)

an origami swan

Origami has delighted and frustrated enthusiasts over the centuries. In fact, today there are many international origami societies established in Britain, Belgium, France, Italy, Japan, the Netherlands, New Zealand, Peru, Spain, and the United States.[2]

In creating an origami figure, the origamist begins with a square sheet of paper and transforms it into any shape limited only by his or her imagination, skill and determination.

A square was probably chosen as the original starting unit of origami because it possesses 4 lines of symmetry, unlike the rectangle or other quadrilaterals. Although some other regular polygons and circles have more lines of symmetry, they lack the right angles of the square, and would have been more difficult to manufacture. Sometimes origamists do begin with other units, but the purists work with squares without using glue or scissors.

In the book *Folding the Universe*, author Peter Engel, a master of the art and science of origami, reveals his years of work, unique discoveries and creations in origami. Engel has taken origami to a whole new plateau, which emphasizes the strong connection between origami, mathematics, and nature by drawing analogies to minimization problems, fractals and the chaos theory. An origami creation begins with a finite amount of material (e.g. a square of fixed dimensions) and evolves into a desired form, not unlike the restrictions placed upon nature in the formation of natural forms, such as bubbles.

Origami is experiencing a renaissance. It has come a long way from the foundations developed by early paperfolders. The complexity of the figures folded by today's masters are truly amazing. Their skill in transforming a square sheet of paper, without the use of scissors or glue, is incredible. The completed forms are not simple boxes or flowers, but anatomically accurate animals, realistic lifelike paper sculptures— squid, spiders, snakes, dancers, furniture. To achieve such proficiency and creativity takes years of work, experience and study — it is analogous to the years which artists like M.C. Escher devoted to developing the art of tessellation. The mathematics, whether identified as such by origamists, is there. Like tessellation art, the understanding of mathematics enhances one's ability and creativity.

Students explore, investigate and discover the precision, excitement and joy of mathematics as they unfold a *Math in Motion* model of the origami box.

A study of the creases impressed on the square sheet of paper, after an origami object has been created, reveals a wealth of geometric objects and properties.

This diagram shows the creases that were impressed on a square when it was folded into a flying bird.

The creases on a square can illustrate the mathematical ideas of similarities, lines and points of symmetry, congruences, ratio and proportions of shapes, and iterations

(continual repetitions of patterns within patterns) resembling the formation of geometric fractals.

Studying the progression of an origami creation is very enlightening. One begins with a square (a 2-dimensional object), and then manipulates the square to form a figure (a 3-dimensional object). If it is a new creation, the origamist will unfold the figure and study the creases impressed on the square. This process involves moving between dimensions. The creases represent the object's 2-dimensional projection onto a flat plane, namely the square. A transformation of a 2-D object to a 3-D object and back is related to the field of projective geometry.

[1] Topology is a special kind of geometry that studies properties of an object that remain unchanged when the object is distorted by being stretched or shrunk. Unlike Euclidean geometry, topology does not deal with size, shape or rigid figures. This is why topology is often referred to as rubber sheet geometry. Imagine objects existing on a rubber sheet that can be stretched and shrunk. In the process of these transformations, one studies the characteristics that remain unchanged.

[2] The Friends of Origami Center of America is located at 15 West 77th St., New York, NY 10024,

[3] Math in Motion is located at 2417 Vista Hogar, Newport Beach, CA 92660 (714) 721-0633.

*From The Mathematics Calendar 1991 and More Joy of Mathematics by Theoni Pappas.
©1991. Reprinted by permission of Wide World Publishing/Tetra, San Carlos, CA.*

Careers & Choices Opportunities

∞5∅8x1≤4≥2%6#7@$9÷3πO≠

Many career opportunities are related to mathematics. Not all of these jobs require advanced math skills. Here are some of the rewarding careers that utilize math skills and thinking ability. Choose one of the careers and answer the following questions:

1) What kind of work does this person do?
2) How is math used in this career?
3) What is the salary I could earn in this field?

Accountant	Financial Advisor
Actuary	Geologist
Aerospace Engineer	Meteorologist
Airline Pilot	Navigator
Archeologist	Oceanographer
Architect	Optometrist
Astronaut	Physician
Astronomer	Radiologist
Banker	Scientist
Biologist	Seismologist
Computer Analyst	Surveyor
Dentist	Technical Writer
Engineer	U.S. Navy Officer...

Part II

Fundamentals

*A*ll things are possible until they are proved impossible.

Pearl S. Buck

Educational Benefits of Origami

Language Arts

Recognition of Pictorial Representations and Symbols
Interpret Diagrams
Develop Verbal and Vocabulary Cues
Develop Communication Skills
Develop Reading and Comprehension
Creative Writing Skills--Origami and Storytelling
Illustrate Creative Dramatics with Origami Puppets
Connect Multicultural Children's Literature and Math

Science

Fold Origami Animals, Birds, Insects and Plants
Save the Whales! Fold a Whale and Research Whales and Other Endangered Species
Environment: Recycle Paper Resources
Test if Origami Boats Sail, Cups Hold Water, the Aerodynamics, Velocity and Motion of Paper Airplanes
Promote Scientific Inquiry: Observe and Measure the Distance of Origami Jumping Frogs

Social Skills

Develop Listening Skills • Following Directions
Develop Precision, Sequence and Organization Skills
Reinforce Concentration, Memory and Recall
Develop Eye-Hand Coordination
Cooperative Learning: Foster Cooperation, Patience and Socialization • Increase Confidence, boosts Self Esteem
Home• School Connection: Encourage Children to Teach Family Members and Friends

Mathematics

Develop Shape, Size, and Color Recognition
Develop Geometric Fundamentals
Develop Math Concepts and Vocabulary
Develop Symmetry • Congruence • Angles
Develop Fractions • Ratio • Proportion
Develop Problem Solving, Analytical, Critical Thinking
Investigate 3-Dimensional Objects • Spatial Sense
Explore Patterns and Make Connections

Social Studies

Increase Multicultural Awareness & Appreciation
Illustrate Historical Events and Holidays
Fold and Send Cranes to Hiroshima, Japan on Peace Day, August 6 (anniversary of the bombing)
Write an Asian Pen-Pal
Explore the Language, Music and History of the East
Promote Peace Education
Fold a Wolf! Learn How to Protect and Conserve Wildlife

Art

Nurture Creativity and Challenge Imagination
Explore Original Ideas Using Origami: Mobiles, Jewlery, Panoramas, Ornaments, Party Decorations
Experiment with Different Textures and Designs of Materials: Recycle Gift Wrap, Magazines, Newspapers, Greeting Cards, Posters, Flyers, Maps and Calendars
Create Variations of Small and Large Models
Decorate a Bulletin Board • Seasonal

Square Power

Establish an environment that allows and encourages risk taking; be sure it is a "safe" place to investigate ideas and to try them out. Examine the folds made from a single sheet of square paper. These are simple folds requiring no special creativity or skill; but if you apply your imagination you will be able to see in them many different shapes and forms.

Roger von Oech, *A Whack on the Side of the Head: How You Can Be More Creative*, states, "In the ten year period between kindergarten and high school, not only had we learned how to find the right answer, we had lost the ability to look for more than one right answer. We had learned how to be specific, but we had lost much of our imaginative power." As noted educator, Neil Postman, remarked, "Children enter schools as question marks and leave as periods."

Invite your students to take a plain square sheet of paper and see how many shapes they can create. What do they see...kites, ice-cream cones, diamonds, books, mountains, birds, butterflies or spaceships? Turn the paper in different directions and examine it from different angles. List how many objects they can find.

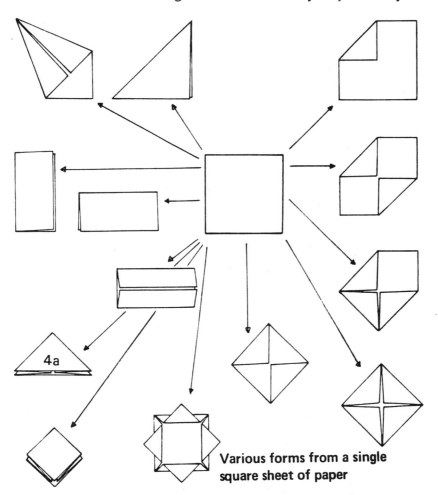

Various forms from a single square sheet of paper

Folding Concepts

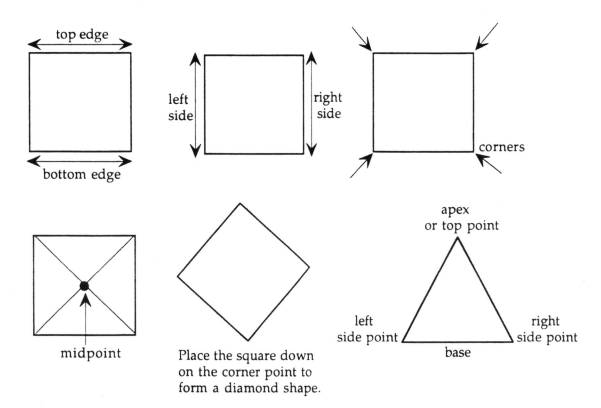

top edge

bottom edge

left side

right side

corners

midpoint

apex
or top point

left
side point

right
side point

base

Place the square down
on the corner point to
form a diamond shape.

Spatial

upper	lower
top	bottom
front	back
inside	outside
outer	inner
beside	behind
center	between
point	midpoint
side	edge
right	left
up	down
forward	backward
opposite	underneath
toward	away from
upward	downward
corner	upside down

Action (verbs)

fold
unfold
push
pull
crease
press
pinch
tuck
open
close
lift
lower
reverse
repeat
sink
pleat

Study the patterns below. The four fundamental bases--kite, fish, bird and frog are related geometrically. The kite base is demonstrated in the whale model (see *Whale* diagram). The other bases involve more advanced techniques. Challenge students to create their own patterns and explore, discover, investigate analyze, and compare their own geometric designs.

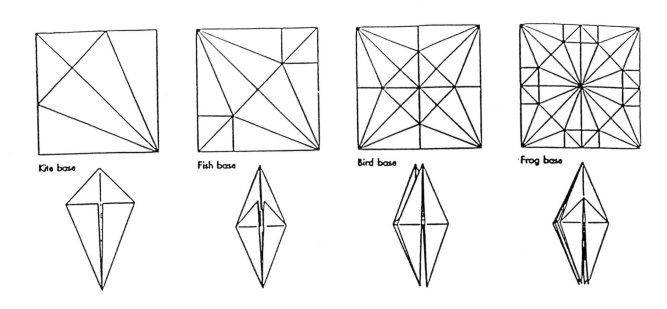

Kite base   Fish base   Bird base   Frog base

Geometry	Quantitative	Qualitative
polygons	length	smooth
square	width	texture
rectangle	height	thick
triangle	area	thin
octagon	volume	plain
trapezoid	perimeter	pattern
parallel		
perpendicular		
bisect		
intersect		
congruent		
angle		
isosceles right triangle		
quadrilateral		
3-dimensional		

Enter the Fold
*Analyzing An Origami Diagram

Materials: Paper • pencil • ruler (see *How to Make a Square*)
Students can use notebook paper to make squares.
Alternative: Precut squares. Give each group 4 squares.
Instructions: Copy *Diagram for First Folds* on the board. Use this exercise to introduce or reinforce shape recognition, math vocabulary and concepts. Students fold and analyze each square pattern. (Younger students can copy the square patterns on their paper squares.) List observations on the squares or discuss responses and write them on the board. See some responses below.

   *Note to Teachers: Probe children's thinking when they respond. Ask: "What can we say about the shape we see? Does anyone have another explanation? Why do you think that? Does anyone have a different way to think about the problem?" Analyzing an origami diagram encourages problem solving and analytical thinking skills. Students discover there can be *more than one* right answer and *more than one* way of looking at a problem.

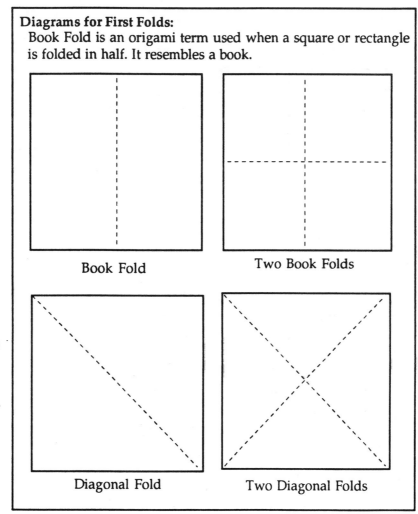

Diagrams for First Folds:
   Book Fold is an origami term used when a square or rectangle is folded in half. It resembles a book.

1. The square is divided into 2 rectangles.
2. The vertical line is the line of symmetry.
3. The lines are parallel.

Book Fold

1. The square is divided into 4 squares.
2. There are 5 squares.
3. The lines form perpendicular lines.

Two Book Folds

1. The square is divided into 2 triangles.
2. The triangles are the same size (congruent).
3. The triangles are isosceles right triangles.

Diagonal Fold

1. The square is divided into 4 triangles.
2. Each triangle is 1/4 of the square.
3. The lines form perpendicular lines.

Two Diagonal Folds

Challenge Page...The Next Fold

Here are more challenging folds to explore. Try folding the square patterns.
List five responses or more for each square and compare your observations.
Space is provided for your answers.

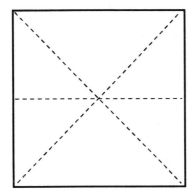

Two diagonals and one book fold.

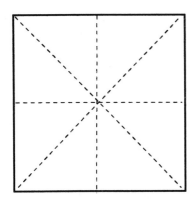

Two diagonals and two book folds.

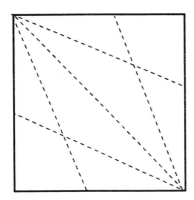

One diagonal whose four angles
are bisected by folds.

Part III

Techniques

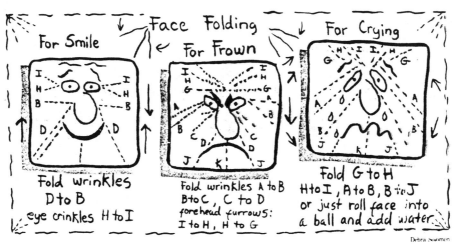

For Smile

Face Folding

For Frown

For Crying

Fold wrinkles
D to B
eye crinkles H to I

Fold wrinkles A to B
B to C, C to D
forehead furrows:
I to H, H to G

Fold G to H
H to I, A to B, B to J
or just roll face into
a ball and add water

Debra Solomon

*O*rigami is in[creasing].

Origami USA

Principles of Paper Folding

Patience

Patience means the willingness to take the time to learn a new skill.
The results are worth the effort.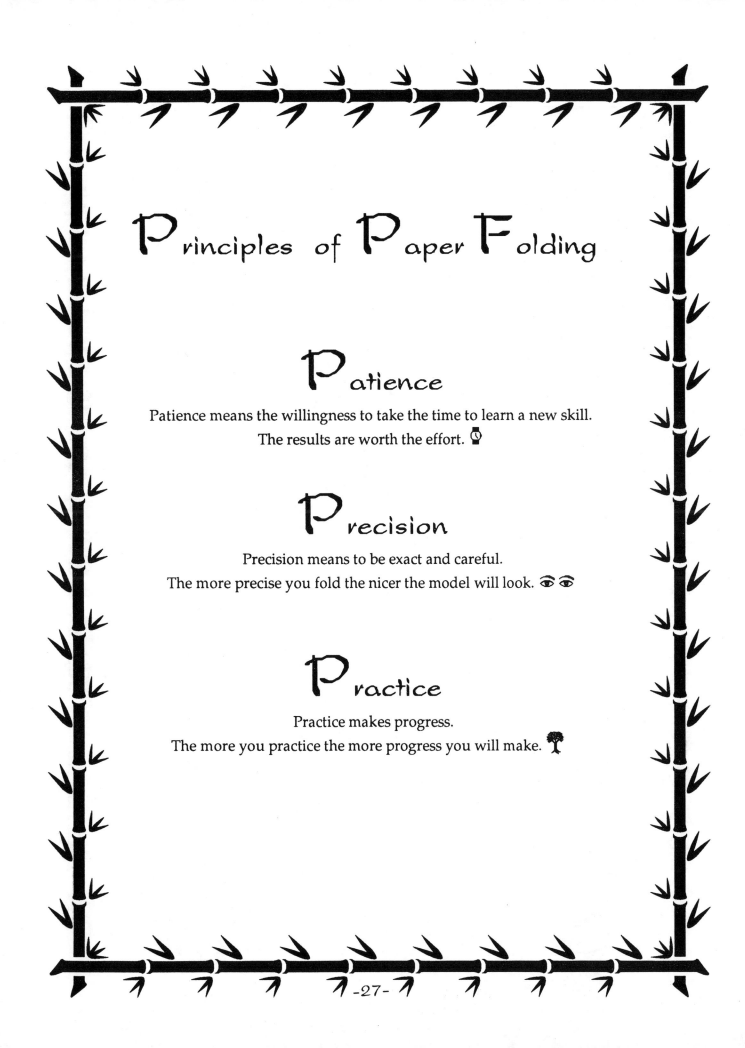

Precision

Precision means to be exact and careful.
The more precise you fold the nicer the model will look.

Practice

Practice makes progress.
The more you practice the more progress you will make.

Paper Resources
(Budget $ Friendly)

Traditional origami paper is precut into squares ranging in sizes, colors and patterns. It is usually colored on one side and white on the other side. For beginners, the larger 6-to 8-inch squares are easier to manipulate.

There are a number of FREE materials that you can recycle. Visit travel agencies and ask for dated travel brochures; video stores for movie posters; garage sales for colorful magazines and maps. Start a Recycling Resource Center in your classroom. Ask students and parents to donate paper from home and work.

Try experimenting with a variety of papers or create your own patterns on a computer (see *Pattern Prints*). Some materials will work better than others depending on the model you are folding. Use practice papers until you are familiar with the design and then have **fun** choosing papers that will enhance your model. Some suggestions include: newspapers, magazines, maps, gift wrap, calendars, book covers, comic books, flyers, junk mail, posters, wall, construction, photocopy, typing, notebook, and computer paper, index cards, telephone books, bags, menus, napkins, paint color chips, business and greeting cards, tax forms, photographs, stamps, coupons, tickets, labels, gum wrappers, travel brochures, programs, announcements, postcards...

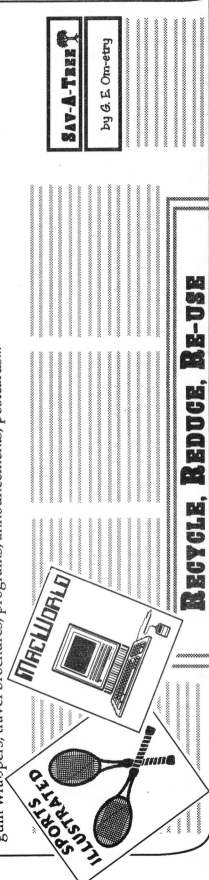

RECYCLE, REDUCE, RE-USE

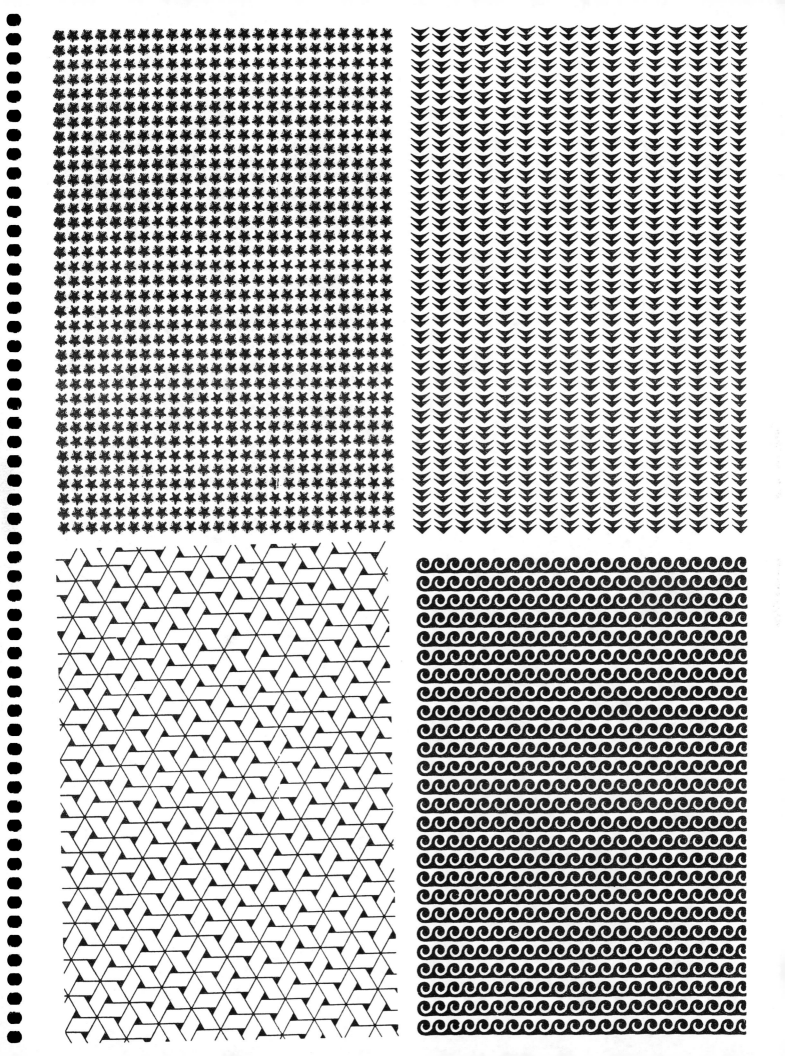

Ten
Teaching
Techniques

1. Begin with a simple model. Place yourself where all the students can see your hands and the sample. If not everyone can see you at once, repeat the step for each side of the room. Encourage students to *observe* your demonstration of a step before they attempt it.

2. Choose large paper to demonstrate. Your sample should be large enough to be seen from the back row, but not too large to manipulate. Highlight or color the lines on *your* model using different color markers or crayons.

3. Fold on a firm surface like a table or a book. Emphasize folding neatly and accurately. Crease each step sharply at least *three* times. The sharper the creases, the easier it will be to see and follow the guidelines.

4. Try to ensure that your students are quiet and attentive. Students must be able to listen and follow directions in a *supportive* learning environment.

5. Encourage students to explore the qualitative and quantitative characteristics of the materials and shapes they use. Ask: "What can we say about the shape we see? How does this material feel?" This open ended question approach encourages students to analyze the figure without the *pressure* of obtaining one right answer. It also enables the teacher to assess what the class already knows.

6. While presenting each step, introduce math concepts and vocabulary (see *Concepts and Vocabulary* for each model) so that your students learn them in context and *experience* them concretely. Have students identify and label each part of the model on their paper.

7. When describing a fold, mention the place where the fold begins and ends, or other "landmarks". Orient your sample the same way your students are folding. Treat each step as one unit: first identify the present position and orientation of the model, perform the step, and then confirm the new position. Make sure each of your students has performed this step correctly. If you sense any uncertainty, repeat your instructions. Try to find a clearer explanation. If a step is challenging, ask students to hold their papers up to check the whole class or *encourage* them to help each other.

8. Avoid folding the student's model. Frustration and failure may alienate them from trying. Establish that a raised hand signals a sign for help without disturbing others. Help individual students or assign another student to assist them. If you have to perform the step on their model, unfold it and let them try again. *Self satisfaction* is very important. If they are still unable to perform the step, you may need to fold their model to enable them to complete it. With practice, they will tout de suite (quickly) develop the confidence they need to succeed.

9. Be supportive and non threatening in your instructions and corrections. Everyone learns at a different pace. Some students may seem more cautious than others and may be afraid to fail and make mistakes. Give the class as much assurance and *positive* encouragement as possible.

10. Have f^{u}n!

May the fold be with you...

Part IV

Teaching Guidelines

(Please Review before Teaching)

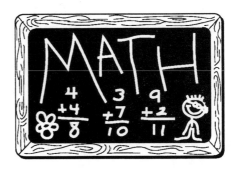

*That's the way things come clear. All of a sudden.
And then you realize how obvious they're been all along.*
Madeleine L'Engle, The Arm of the Starfish

Lesson Plan Guide

The math-oriented curriculum was developed to provide the classroom teacher or specialist with a general framework to support National Standards and curriculum requirements. Many of the activities were chosen to provide specific activities in the development of the elementary students' auditory, verbal, visual and motor growth. In addition four of the models (*Box, *Frog, *Whale and *Dog) in *How to Fold...* demonstrate questions formulated specifically for the math class. See ***Teacher Scripts** in the *Table of Contents*. The professional is encouraged to expand or modify these activities according to the students' capabilities.

Objectives:

- **To develop auditory and visual attention skills** (listening and following directions)

- **To develop visual-motor skills** (eye-hand coordination)

- **To develop temporal-spatial concepts** (the ability to understand the position of the self and objects with relation to each other)

- **To develop shape, size, color and pattern recognition** (exploring investigating, making connections, identifying, creating, communicating)

- **To develop sequencing skills** (retain and recall information in appropriate order)

- **To develop basic geometric principles** (concrete models, constructing and deconstructing, relationships, patterns, vocabulary and concepts)

- **To integrate math with other subjects** (Language Arts, Social Studies, Science, Music, Technology, Art, Dramatic Play, Literature, Storytelling, Multicultural Education)

- **To develop awareness and appreciation for cultural diversity** (respect and tolerance)

Procedure

Before folding the models in this book, review *Ten Teaching Techniques.* Study Parts II and III, *Fundamentals and Techniques.* As you become familiar with teaching the model, refer to these sections whenever necessary to expand the lesson. The models are divided into three groups, *Models Made from Rectangles, Models Made from Squares and Models Made from Triangles.* The models range in complexity from simple to intermediate and are presented in that order, although there is some variation within each group.

Save paper. Some of the activities and exercises can be transferred to an overhead or drawn on the chalkboard. Students can use their notebook paper, journals or other recycled materials. Select a few concepts to teach at one time. Model the process step by step. At each step, introduce or review the *Concepts and Vocabulary* for each project. During the lesson encourage divergent thinking by asking, "What can we say about the shape we see?" Divergent thinking challenges students to consider a myriad of possibilities, alternatives and consequences. This open-ended question approach encourages students to analyze the figure without the pressure of obtaining *one* right answer. It also enables the teacher to assess what the class already knows.

Ask students to write the vocabulary word and its definition on the part of the paper that represents that term. For younger children, work in small groups and introduce some of the new vocabulary words and concepts like quadrilateral and symmetry. Write the words on the board as they trace the place on the paper with their fingers. *Having the information go in your ears and out of your hands helps you learn it.* When students get to feel, touch and see the concepts being taught, it reinforces learning and enhances memory and recall. See *Additional Activities* for more suggestions and ideas to extend the lesson.

> ***Helpful Hints: Emphasize the rules**
> **1. Fold precisely. (neatly and accurately)**
> **2. Crease sharlply!**

*Remember every fold is a <u>guideline</u>. It guides you to the next place on the paper. Origami folds are communicated through drawings showing the progression of the fold as well as verbal instructions. Each drawing shows two things: *the result of the previous step,* and *what action is next.* Before folding the next step shown, *look* 👁 👁 ahead to see what the result will be. The more precise you fold, the nicer the model will look. The sharper you crease, the easier it will be to SEE the guidelines.

Cross-Reference Chart

Math in Motion

	Mathematics	Language Arts	Reading	Social Studies	Science	Animals	H$_2$O	Holidays	Seasons	Transportation
Box										
Candy Cane										
Cat										
Cup										
Dog										
Fish										
Heart										
Jumping Frog										
Picture Frame										
Pig										
Journal										
Sailboat										
Sailor's Hat										
Tulip										
Whale										
Wolf										

Marked cells (indicated by apple icons):

- **Box:** Mathematics, Language Arts, Reading, Holidays
- **Candy Cane:** Mathematics, Language Arts, Reading, Holidays
- **Cat:** Mathematics, Language Arts, Reading, Science, Animals, Holidays
- **Cup:** Mathematics, Language Arts, Reading, Holidays
- **Dog:** Mathematics, Language Arts, Reading, Science, Animals
- **Fish:** Mathematics, Language Arts, Reading, Science, Animals, H$_2$O
- **Heart:** Mathematics, Language Arts, Reading, Holidays
- **Jumping Frog:** Mathematics, Language Arts, Reading, Science, Animals, H$_2$O
- **Picture Frame:** Mathematics, Language Arts, Reading, Holidays
- **Pig:** Mathematics, Language Arts, Reading, Science, Animals
- **Journal:** Mathematics, Language Arts, Reading
- **Sailboat:** Mathematics, Language Arts, Reading, Social Studies, Science, Holidays, Transportation
- **Sailor's Hat:** Mathematics, Language Arts, Reading, Social Studies
- **Tulip:** Mathematics, Language Arts, Reading, Science, Seasons
- **Whale:** Mathematics, Language Arts, Reading, Science, Animals, H$_2$O
- **Wolf:** Mathematics, Language Arts, Reading, Science, Animals, H$_2$O

Origami isn't Just for Squares

Math in Motion uses three basic geometric ▌□▲ shapes in paperfolding projects--rectangles, squares and triangles.

Models Made from Rectangles...the shape of this page can also be made from student notebook or duplicating paper. There are many sources of rectangular shapes to recycle (see *Paper Resources*).

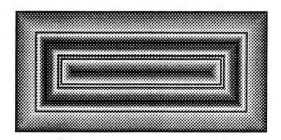

Models Made from Squares...are the most traditional shape used for origami. Use a paper cutter to trim the paper precisely into a square shape or make the square from a rectangle (see *How to Make a Square from a Rectangle*).

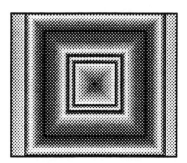

Models Made from Triangles...often start with an isosceles right triangle. Isosceles right triangles have two sides the same length. Right triangles have one square corner. Isosceles right triangles have both (see *How to Make an Isosceles Right Triangle*).

Part V

Paper Folding
Projects

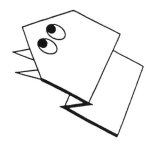

*I*f you can dream it, you can make it so.

Belva Davis

Symbols

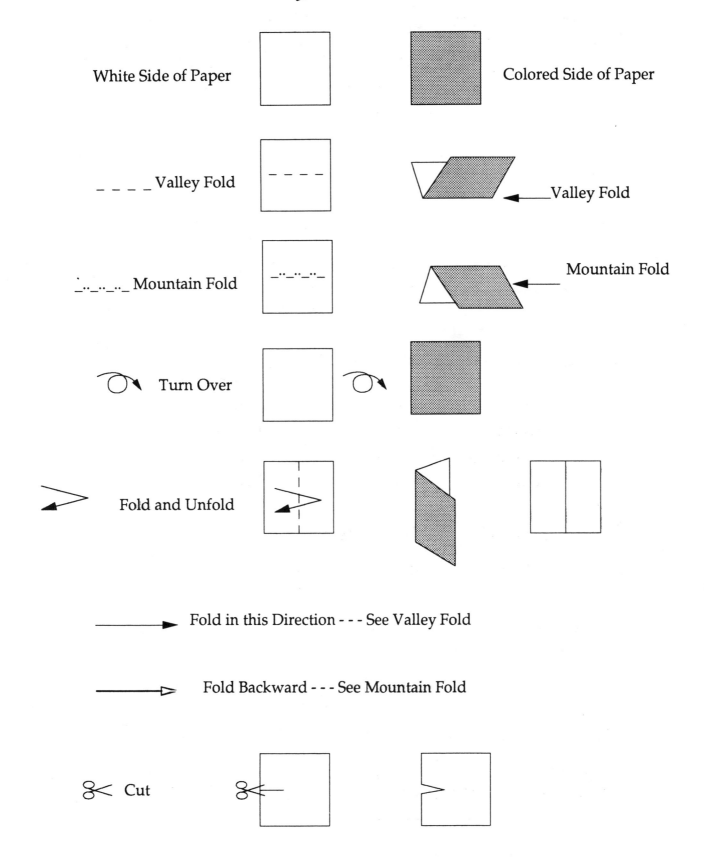

White Side of Paper

Colored Side of Paper

_ _ _ _ Valley Fold

Valley Fold

_.._.._.._ Mountain Fold

Mountain Fold

Turn Over

Fold and Unfold

Fold in this Direction - - - See Valley Fold

Fold Backward - - - See Mountain Fold

Cut

Heart

This model is easy. Practice random acts of kindness. Send ✉ hearts to a sister school, nursing home or Peace Pal (see Resources, *The Global Link Newsletter*).

Strand: Geometry • Shape Recognition • Spatial Sense

Materials: A red or pink rectangle, 8-1/2-inch x 2-1/2-inch
Alternative: Use the strip left over after you make a square from an 8-1/2-inch by 11-inch rectangle. (See *How to Make a Square from a Rectangle*).

Concepts and Vocabulary:

rectangle	pentagon	isosceles right triangle
apex	base	length
width	vertical	line of symmetry
congruent	edge	corner
right left	top	bottom

Additional Activities:

1. See *How to Fold the Dog* and *Box* models to extend the *Concepts and Vocabulary* lessons on the triangle and rectangle.

2. Make several *Math in Motion* hearts of different sizes. Glue them together. Teach the concept of small, smaller, smallest. ♥♥♥

3. Make a heart for Valentine's Day. Write a heartfelt message inside. Write poems of love and friendship and attach it to the heart.

4. For St. Patrick's Day, make three green hearts to form a shamrock. ☘

5. Write Love Notes. Reinforce communication between parents and children. Tape the ♥ to the child's shirt with a message inside. "Ask me how my day went" or "Tell me how much I mean to you." Make it a weekly event.

Heart

1 Start with a rectangle, white side up. Place on the table with the length (long edges) at the top and bottom. Fold the left side over to meet the right side (book fold). Unfold.

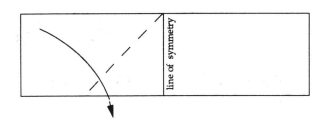

2 Fold the top left edge down to meet the line of symmetry (center crease).

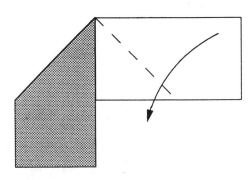

3 Fold the top right edge down to meet the center crease.

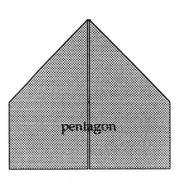

4 It looks like a tent. Turn over.

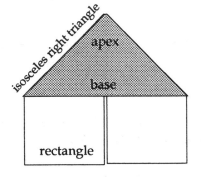

5 Now it looks like a house.

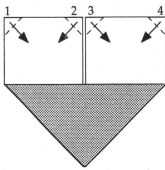

6 Turn the top around to the bottom. See the four corners at the top. Fold each corner down into a small triangle.

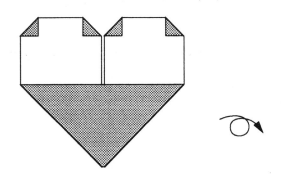

7 Now it looks like this. Turn over.

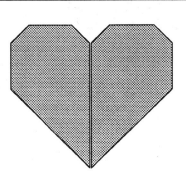

8 Write a special message inside. Give your heart to art!

Sailor's Hat

You can wear this model. Have a parade or a fashion show.

Strand: Geometry • Spatial Sense • Literature

Materials: 8-1/2-inch x 11-inch rectangle (notebook or bond paper).
Alternative: Make a newspaper hat you can wear (see *Additional Activities*).

Concepts and Vocabulary:

rectangle	side	quadrilateral
right	left	line of symmetry
vertical line	apex	base
pentagon	triangle	isosceles right triangle
bottom	edge	right angle

Additional Activities:

1. Make the sailor's ⚓ hat out of newspaper to fit your head. Use a standard single sheet of newspaper approximately 22-inch x 13-inch. Ask parents and neighbors to save the Sunday comics. **Hint:** Newspaper is springy, crease sharply!

2. Be creative. Decorate a hat. Provide a wide range of materials. Glue on sequins, beads, felt, ribbon, lace, velvet, pipe cleaners, noodles, 'bubble' packing.

3. Write your name, school or team on the front rim of the hat and "I love Math" on the back rim.

4. Turn the hat upside down, punch holes on the sides and staple yarn or string as a strap for a shoulder bag.

5. Read *Curious George Rides a Bike* by H. A. Rey. Discover how to recycle your hat into a boat (instructions included).

Sailor's Hat

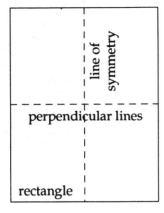

1 Start with an 8.5" x 11" rectangle or sheet of newspaper, approximately 22" x 13". Fold in half lengthwise. Unfold. Fold in half crosswise.

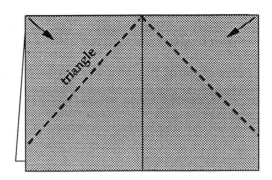

2 Fold outer corners along diagonal dotted lines to meet at the centerline.

Fold this step if using 8.5" x 11" paper.

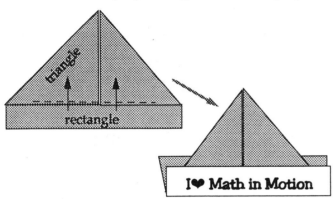

3 Fold TOP LAYER OF PAPER ONLY, along the bottom edge of the horizontal dotted line over triangles. Repeat on the other side. Your hat is now finished!

Fold steps 3-5 to make a newspaper hat you can wear.

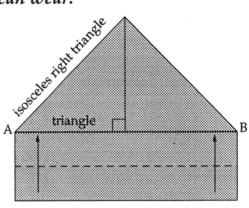

3 Fold TOP LAYER OF PAPER ONLY, along the bottom edge of the horizontal dotted line up to points A and B (see arrows).

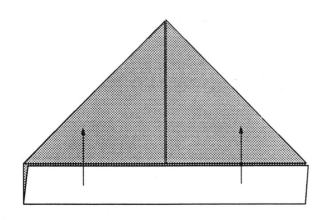

4 Fold the bottom edge up again over the triangles to lock in place. Turn the hat over and repeat steps 3 and 4 on the other side.

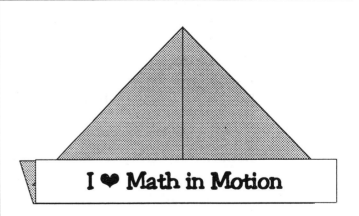

5 Aye, aye, Captain! Your newspaper hat is ready to wear.

Box

This model was traditionally known as the "magazine box". Make two the same size and connect them together. Use for storage or display.

Strand: Fractions • Geometry

Materials: Two rectangles, 8-1/2-inch by 11-inch (duplicating paper).
Alternative: Recycle. Use the front and back covers of magazines.

Concepts and Vocabulary

Fractions		Geometry	
whole	1	rectangle	perpendicular lines
halves	1/2	quadrilateral	isosceles right triangle
quarters	1/4	triangle	octagon
eighths	1/8	length	width
sixteenths	1/16	parallel lines	line of symmetry

Additional Activities:

1. Measure the length, width, and height of the box. Calculate the area and volume.

    A. What is the area of the box? Area is measured in square units.
        $A = L \times W$ (Area = Length x Width)
    B. What is the volume of the box? Volume is measured in cubic units.
        $V = L \times W \times H$ (Volume = Length x Width x Height)

2. Create three boxes of varying sizes. Who can make the smallest box? Largest? Calculate the area and volume of each box based on the size of the paper. Record your findings in a table. Summarize the results. Can you predict how to change the dimensions so that the area and volume are increased? Decreased?

3. Make a basket. Fold a piece of paper lengthwise and staple a handle to the sides.

4. Draw a picture on the cover of the box. Decorate with markers or make a collage. Write a poem or story about the picture and glue it inside the base of the box.

Box

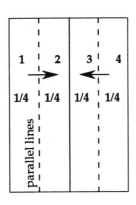

1 Start with a rectangle, white side up. Fold in half length-wise (book fold). Unfold.

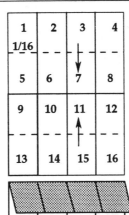

2 Bring longer edges to meet at the center crease (cupboard door fold).

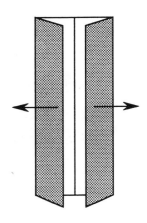

3 Unfold.

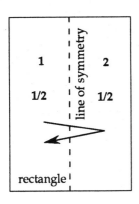

4 Fold in half widthwise (book fold). Unfold.

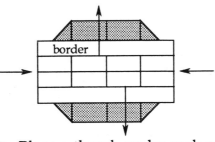

5 Bring shorter edges to meet at the center crease. This time leave the folds in.

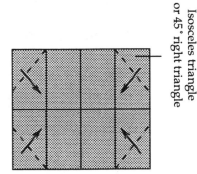

Isosceles triangle or 45° right triangle

6 At each corner, bring the folded edge to lie along the nearest crease to form a triangle.
Note: Cut edges do **NOT** reach the centerline.

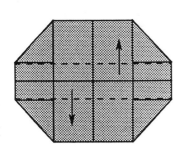

7 Fold the cut edges, one up and one down, as far as you can over the corner triangles to hold them down in place.

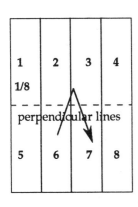

8 Place a thumb under each of the rectangular borders and pull them apart. The ends of the model will fold upward to become the sides of a box. Pinch the corners of the box to shape them square.

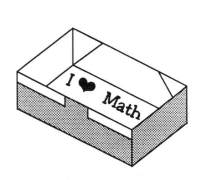

9 Voilà! A finished box! Make another for a lid.

How to Fold the Box

1. Fold the **whole** rectangle in half lengthwise. Unfold.

What is a rectangle?	A **quadrilateral** that has four right angles.
What is a right angle?	A right angle measures 90°.
What is a quadrilateral?	A quadrilateral has four sides.
Name other quadrilaterals.	Square, rhombus, parallelogram, trapezoid.
What kind of line is it?	**Line of symmetry.**
What is a line of symmetry?	A line of folding so that the two parts of a figure match (congruent).

Younger children can write numerals in each part. Write the numbers 1 and 2. Draw two objects, stars or apples to correspond with the number (one to one correspondence). Older children can write fractions in each part. Write the faction 1/2. Discuss the parts of a fraction. **Numerator:** Tells how many parts you are talking about. In 3/4, 3 is the numerator. **Denominator:** Total number of parts or groups. In 3/4, 4 is the denominator.

2. Fold lengthwise. Unfold.

How many equal parts?	Four. Write 1/4 in each section.
What kind of lines do you see?	Vertical lines.
What is another name for the lines?	Parallel lines.
What are parallel lines?	Lines that never intersect, cross or meet.

4. Fold in half crosswise. Unfold.

What kind of lines do you see?	Perpendicular lines. Trace the lines.
What are perpendicular lines?	Lines that intersect and form right angles.
How many equal parts is the paper divided into?	Eight. Write 1/8 in each section.

5. Fold crosswise. Unfold. Discover a grid. The grid offers many opportunities to explore and investigate number relationships and patterns like counting, place value, symbol recognition, and comparing. Analyze the data and graph the results.

When the paper is unfolded, how many parts do you see?	Sixteen. Write 1/16 in each part.
How many rectangles can you find?	100.

Write the numerals 1-16 horizontally in each box. Younger children can practice counting backwards, forwards, skip counting by 2's, and 4's. Add up rows and columns. Multiply. Calculate mentally, with a pencil or use a calculator.

Circle the even numbers.　　　　　　　　　　2, 4, 6, 8, 10, 12, 14, 16.

Put a square around the odd numbers.　　　　1, 3, 5, 7, 9, 11, 13, 15.

Name or write the next ten numbers　　　　Even: 18, 20, 22, 24, 26, 28, 30, 32, 34, 36.
in each series.　　　　　　　　　　　　　　Odd:　17, 19, 21, 23, 25, 27, 29, 31, 33, 35.

Discover even + even numbers will always give an even number, 2 + 4 = 6.
Even + odd numbers will always give an odd number, 2 + 3 = 5.
Odd + odd numbers will always give an even number, 3 + 5 = 8.
Allow students to experiment, test, make predictions and prove their work.
Ask students to draw or write about how they would explain it. Share reports.

Discuss prime and composite numbers. One is neither prime nor composite?

What is a prime number?　　　　　　　　A prime number has exactly two
　　　　　　　　　　　　　　　　　　　　different factors.

Place the letter "P" over all　　　　　　　2, 3, 5, 7, 11, 13.
the prime numbers.

What is a composite number?　　　　　　A composite number has more than
　　　　　　　　　　　　　　　　　　　　two factors.

Place the letter "C" over all　　　　　　　4, 6, 8, 9, 10, 12, 14, 15, 16.
the composite numbers.

Investigate number patterns vertically and diagonally. Look at the vertical number pattern 1, 5, 9, and 13 on the grid.

What is the pattern?　　　　　　　　　　They increase by 4.

Name or write the next 10 numbers　　　　17, 21, 25, 29, 33, 37, 41, 45, 49 53.
in the series. Look for other patterns.

Compare numbers. Explore greater than and less than. Write 5 number sentences. Use the greater than > and less than < symbols. **Ex:** Seven is less than nine. 7 < 9.

6. Refold to step 5. At each corner, bring the folded edge to lie along the nearest crease line. **Note** that the cut edges **DO NOT** reach the crosswise centerline.

What shape do you see? What kind?　　　Triangle. Isosceles right triangle.

How many sides does this shape have?　　Eight.

What is this shape?　　　　　　　　　　Octagon.

7. Fold the rectangular borders over the triangles. Repeat on the other side.

8. GENTLY open and fold back the borders. Pinch the corners of the box to shape.

9. Voila! A finished box. Make another one the same size for a lid. Connect.

Journal

This model is suitable for all ages. The final assembly can be challenging.

Strand: Geometry • Spatial Sense

Materials: 8-1/2-inch by 11-inch rectangle (notebook or copy paper)
Scissors ✂

Concepts and Vocabulary:

rectangle	quadrilateral	line of symmetry
vertical line	length	width
fractions	whole	halves
quarters	eighths	perpendicular lines
right angle	midpoint	edge

Additional Activities:

1. See *How to fold a Box* to extend lessons for the rectangle.

2. Make an invitation for "Back to School Night".

3. Use it for journal writing in the class: math journal (writing numerals, number facts and multiplication tables) creative writing, sketching, poetry, spelling lists, and homework assignments. See *Journal Writing*.

4. For younger children, use the journal as a picture word book. Draw or paste a picture above the new words.

5. List all the ways one uses numbers and illustrate: tell time, count change, weigh and measure, address, zip code, area code, telephone number. Celebrate Mathematics Education Month during the month of April. Contact NCTM for more ideas and free information about Math Education Month and math related resources. Posters, stickers, videos, books, magazines and more. Ask for a catalog.

National Council of Teachers of Mathematics (NCTM)
1906 Association Drive
Reston, Virginia 22091
☎ 1-800-235-7566

Journal

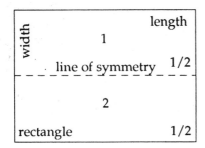

width		length
	1	
line of symmetry		1/2
	2	
rectangle		1/2

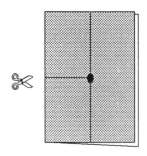

1/4		1/4
1		2
perpendicular lines		
3		4
1/4		1/4

1 Start with a rectangle. Place the length (long edges) at the top and bottom. Fold the bottom edge up to meet the top edge. Unfold.

2 Fold the left side over to meet the right side. Do not unfold.

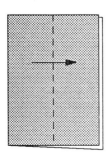

3 Fold the left folded side over to meet the right side.

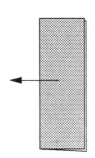

4 Unfold the last step.

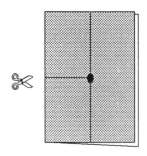

5 Cut along the centerline from the folded side to the midpoint only.

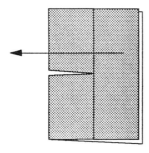

6 Unfold.

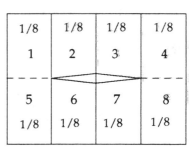

1/8	1/8	1/8	1/8
1	2	3	4
5	6	7	8
1/8	1/8	1/8	1/8

7 Fold the top edge down to the bottom again.

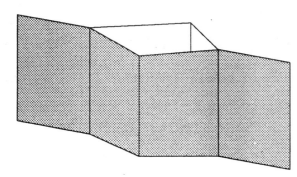

8 Push together to form a book, using the folds you have made.

9 Mathematics + Writing = Success. Write your way into math!

Jumping Frog

This popular action model will delight all ages. It requires more coordination.

Strand: Geometry • Measurement • Language

Materials: 3" x 5" green index card or a stiff rectangle
Alternative: After students master the larger index cards, challenge them with smaller cards like business size cards or paint chips.

Concepts and Vocabulary:

rectangle	triangle	perpendicular lines
plane	intersect	isosceles right triangle
vertical	bisect	pentagon
line segment	right angle	apex
side	point	base

Additional Activities:

1. Fold the box model. Make the frog jump in the box. Give two points for every jump *in* the box. Side. Over. Make up a point system and tally your score.

2. There are almost 4,000 different kinds of frogs and toads in the world. The goliath frog is the world's largest with a body as big as a football. One of the smallest frogs found in the Cuban Rain Forests is no bigger than the eraser on your pencil! Visit the library and find out more about these leaping amphibians.

3. Scientist from all over the world recently realized there are far fewer frogs than ever before. Frogs need puddles and ponds to hatch their eggs, but these places are often polluted. Learn how you can be an Earth Saver. Start a *Kids for Saving Earth Club* at your school (see Resources, *Earth Savers*).

4. Read Mark Twain's, *The Jumping Frog of Calavaras County* (cassette available) The longest recorded jump is 6ft. 7in. (1.78m). Test your frog's jumping skills. Organize a Frog Jumping Olympics. Use masking tape to set up a starting point and finishing line. Measure the length of your jumps and record the best distance out of five. Experiment with different size frogs. Tabulate and graph the results. What size frog jumps the farthest? Create an obstacle course--over mountains of books, miniature ponds created from foil, pencils, and erasers.

Jumping Frog

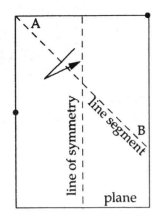

1 Start with a 3" x 5" rectangle. Fold in half lengthwise. Unfold. Fold the top right edge over to the **left edge. Unfold.**

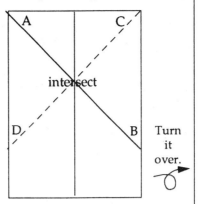

2 Repeat on the other side. Unfold. See the letter 'X.' Turn card over.

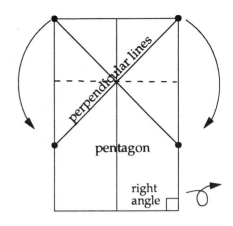

3 Fold the top of the 'X' down to the bottom of the 'X.' Unfold. Turn card over.

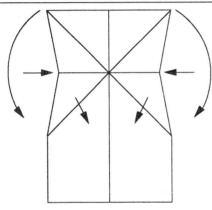

4 Put your finger in the center of the 'X' and the sides will pop up. The whole next move is done on creases made in steps 1-3. Push the sides toward the center (see arrows) as the top collapses into a triangle.

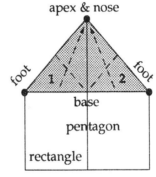

5 Now it looks like a house. The tip of the triangle will be the frog's nose. The two side triangles will be the feet. Fold the side point (foot) of triangle 1 up to the top point (nose) of the triangle. Repeat on triangle 2 to form a square.

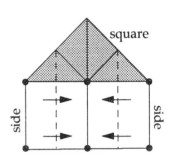

6 Fold the sides of the house onto the centerline. Unfold. Count the triangles. Can you find 11? **FOLD THE SIDES BACK ONTO THE CENTERLINE.**

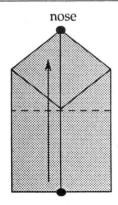

7 GENTLY fold the bottom **edge up to the nose. DO NOT CREASE SHARPLY.** This is **the spring action.**

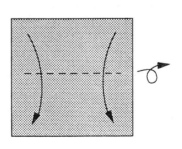

8 GENTLY fold back the top layer only to match the folded edge at the bottom. DO NOT CREASE SHARPLY.

9 To make the frog jump, lightly press down on the frog's back, then let go. Note the letter 'Z' formed by the side edge. This is the spring that causes the frog to jump. Stretch it out and fold back as needed to improve jump.

How to Fold the Jumping Frog

Suggestion: Discuss the characteristics of a **rectangle** and **plane** figure.
A plane is a flat surface that continues infinitely in all directions.
See *How to Fold the Box* to extend the lesson on rectangles.

1. Place the rectangle on the table **vertically.** Fold in half lengthwise. Unfold. Fold the right top edge over to the left edge. Unfold.

What kind of line does this fold create? **Line segment.**

What is a line segment? A line segment is part of a line that begins at one **point** and ends at another point. It is named by its two endpoints. Label it line segment

$\overline{AB}$ or AB.

2. Repeat on the other side. Unfold. Label it line segment CD. See the letter "X".

What kind of lines do $\overline{AB}$ and $\overline{CD}$ form? They form **perpendicular lines**.

What are perpendicular lines? These are lines that **intersect** (meet) and form **right angles**. Trace the lines with your finger to form the letter "X".

How much does a right angle measure? 90°.

How many right angles are there? Twelve. Number all the right angles.

3. Turn the card over. Point to the top of the "X". Point to the bottom of the "X". Take the top of the "X" and fold it down to the bottom of the "X". Unfold. The crease will **bisect** line segments AB and CD or the "X". Turn the card over.

*How many **triangles** are there?* Eleven.

4. Place your finger in the center of the "X" and the sides will pop-up. The whole next move is done on preexisting creases from steps 1-3. Place your index fingertips on the sides of the bisecting line where the arrows are pointing. Push the sides toward the center as the top collapses into a triangle. It looks like a house. See *How to Fold the Dog* to extend the lesson on triangles.

How many sides does this polygon have?   Five.

What is a five sided figure called?   **Pentagon.**

Trace the pentagon with your finger and number the sides.

5. Fold the right side point (foot) of the triangle up to the top point or apex (nose) of the triangle. Repeat on the left side. The tip of the triangle (**apex**) will be the frog's nose. The two triangles on the sides will be its feet.

What shape do these triangles create?   **Square.**

6. Fold the sides of the house onto the center guideline to narrow the card.

7. **WARNING:** DO NOT CREASE STEPS #7 and #8 SHARPLY. GENTLY fold the bottom straight edge of the card up to the apex. This is the spring action that makes the frog jump.

8. GENTLY fold the top edge down in half towards you (creates a pleat) to match the folded edge.

9. To make the frog jump, *lightly* press down on the frog's back and let go. Make two and play leap frog.

How to Make
a Square from a Rectangle

Method #1

Fold the corner to the opposite side to form a triangle.

Cut along the vertical line of the rectangle. **Alternative:** *Without a scissor,* fold the rectangular portion back and forth several times. Place one hand against the triangle. Separate the rectangular portion with the other hand.

The rectangular strip left over can be used for making smaller squares or 1) Use it to make a heart. 2) Fold lengthwise (book fold) to shape a handle. Staple to the sides of the box for a basket.

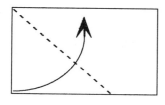

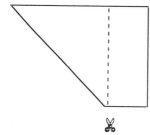

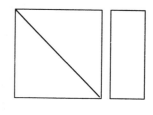

Method #2

For a square without a diagonal crease, place two identical sheets of rectangular paper as shown. Cut the bottom sheet along the raw edge of the top sheet.

The sheet underneath is now square. For a second square, turn both layers over and cut the larger sheet using the raw edge of the square as a guide.

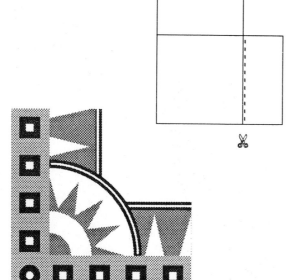

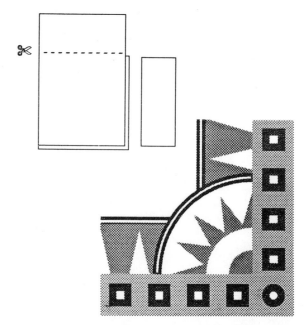

Whale

This fishy model is easy and good for beginners. Have a whale of a time!

Strand: Geometry • Spatial Sense • Patterns • Connections

Materials: Square, 6-inch or larger, white side up

Concepts and Vocabulary:

square	quadrilateral	triangle	scalene triangle
congruent	**vertical**	center	isosceles right triangle
right	left	point	line of symmetry

Additional Activities:

1. How many ways can a **square** be divided into 4 equal parts? See *Square Motion*.

2. Make a whale as a Father's Day card for a "Whale of a Dad." Use as name tags for the first day of school (a school of fish) or "Back to School."

3. Read *A Thousand Pails of Water* by R. Roy, (K-2) and *Humphrey, The Wayward Whale* by E. Callenbach, (K-6) or other stories about fish-like mammals (dolphins).

4. Did you know whales sing? Nobody knows for sure, but perhaps they are singing the blues. Listen to Paul Winter's "Lullaby from the Great Mother Whale for the Baby Seal Pups,"*Concert for the Earth, Live at the United Nations. Younger children will enjoy "Baby Beluga" by *Raffi in Concert*.

5. Adopt a Whale? Write for more information:

   Greenpeace
   1436 U Street, N.W.
   Washington, D.C. 20009
   ☎ 1-800-456-4029

   Save the Whales
   P.O. Box 2397
   Venice, CA 90291
   ☎ 1-800-942-5365

Whale

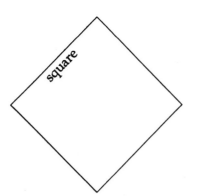

1 Put a square on the table so it looks like a diamond.

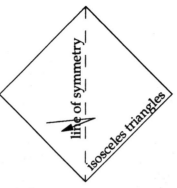

line of symmetry

isosceles triangles

2 Fold the left point over to meet the right point. Unfold. Find the center crease.

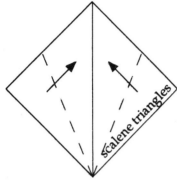

scalene triangles

3 Fold the lower left and right sides to meet the center crease.

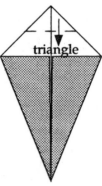

triangle

4 It looks like a kite. Now fold the top point down, as shown to form a small triangle.

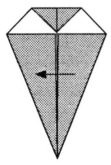

5 Fold the right side over to meet the left side.

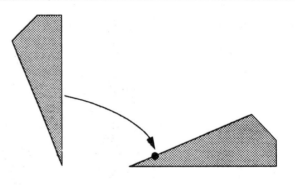

6 Put your finger on the bottom point as you turn the whale sideways.

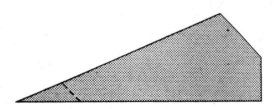

7 Fold the end point up to make a tail.

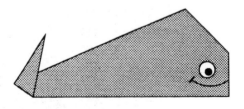

8 Draw a happy face. Have a whale of a day!

How to Fold the Whale

1. Place a square sheet of paper on the table so it looks like a diamond shape.

What shape is the paper?	**Square.**
How many sides does a square have?	**4 sides.**
What else can you say about the sides?	The sides are the same or **congruent.**

Another name for a four sided figure is **quadrilateral** (see *Quadrilaterals*).

Can you think of other quadrilaterals?	Rectangle, parallelogram, rhombus, trapezoid.
Name other quadrilaterals in the room.	Book, desk, window, table, chalkboard.

2. Fold the right point over to the left point. Unfold.

*What is the **center vertical** line?*	**Line of symmetry.**
What is a line of symmetry?	A line of folding so that the two halves of a figure match.
What shapes did it create?	**Triangles.**
What kind of triangles?	**Isosceles right triangles.**
What is an isosceles right triangle?	It has two sides that are congruent.

3. Fold the lower left and right sides to meet the center crease. Unfold the paper and discover...more triangles.

What kind of triangles?	**Scalene** triangles.
What are scalene triangles?	They have no congruent sides.
How many triangles are there?	Six. Refold the model.
What does it look like?	It looks like a kite.

4. Fold the top point down to the widest part of the kite to form a small triangle. ▼ Unfold.

How many triangles are there?	Nine.

5. Refold the model. Fold the **right** side over to meet the **left** side.

6. Put your finger on the bottom point as you turn the whale sideways.

7. Fold the end **point** up to make a tail. Draw a happy face on the whale.

Quadrilateral

Quad-ri-lat-er-al is Latin for a figure that has four sides.
"Quad," means four and "lateral," means side. Find other quadrilaterals.
1) Look for objects in the room that are similar in shape.
2) Trace the geometric shapes below and draw another one.
3) See *Tangram Puzzles* and make a quadrilateral.

1. **Square**-a figure that has four right angles and four sides of equal length. Every square is a rectangle.

2. **Rectangle**-a quadrilateral that has four right angles. Every rectangle is a parallelogram.

3. **Parallelogram**-a quadrilateral that has two pairs of parallel sides and two pairs of congruent sides. Every parallelogram is a trapezoid.

4. **Rhombus**-a parallelogram that has four congruent sides. Every rhombus is a parallelogram.

5. **Trapezoid**-a quadrilateral that has exactly one pair of parallel sides.

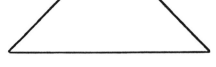

Square Motion

Materials: paper • pencil • ruler • three squares
Note to Teacher: (See *Enter the Fold*)

1. How can a square be divided into four equal parts?
2. Describe the folds and list your observations.
3. Fold the square patterns.
4. Create your own geometric designs.
5. Color the squares.

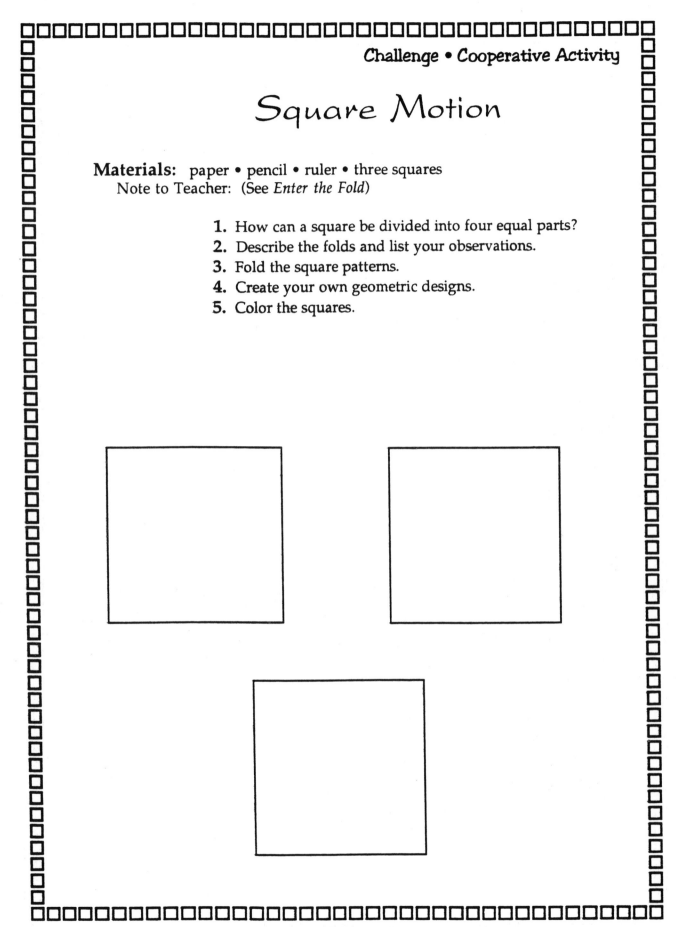

Wolf or Fox

The wolf's ears are challenging. Work in small groups or demonstrate to one child at a table and ask them to assist other children in the group.

Strand: Geometry • Spatial Sense

Materials: A 6-inch or larger square • Crayons or markers

Concepts and Vocabulary:

square	line of symmetry	triangle	right angle
point	isosceles right triangle	edge	side

Additional Activities:

1. Make a wolf mask, using a 12-inch square. Cut out holes for the eyes. 👁 👁 Staple elastic to hold it in place on the child's face.

2. Idioms: This activity develops comprehension of language. Invite students to illustrate the literal and figurative meanings of the following idioms. Make up your own idioms. Display on a bulletin board.

   1. sly as a fox
   2. eat like a bird
   3. let the cat out of the bag
   4. it's raining cats and dogs
   5. quit horsing around
   6. a frog in my throat

3. Sponsor a wolf (canis lupus pambasileuses)! Learn more about what you can do to conserve and protect wildlife. Receive a certificate that includes your wolf's name, photo, biography and bookmark. For more information, contact:

   Wolf Haven International
   3111 Offut Lake Road
   Tenino, Washington 98589
   ☎ 1-800-448-9653

Wolf

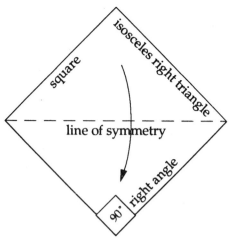

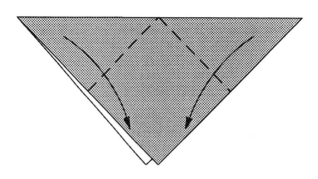

1 Start with a square, white side up so it looks like a diamond. Fold the top point down to meet the bottom point.

2 Fold the left and right points down to meet the bottom point.

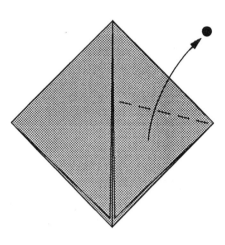

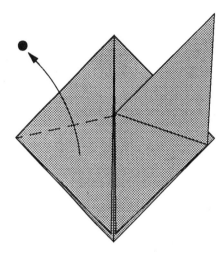

3 Put your index finger on the top point. Fold the lower right point up to the dot to make the ears.

4 Repeat with the lower left point.

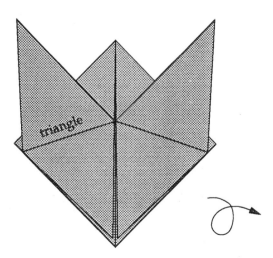

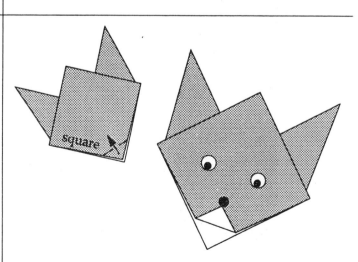

5 Turn over.

6 Look at the lower point. There are two layers. Fold only the top layer up on the dotted line to make the mouth. Draw eyes and nose.

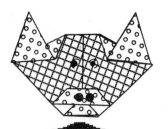
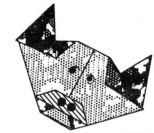

Pig

To open and close the pig's mouth, place your thumbs on its ears and your fingers on the back of its head. Move your hands together and apart.

Strand: Geometry • Spatial Sense

Materials:
A 6-inch square, white side up
Crayons or markers

Concepts and Vocabulary:

square	line of symmetry	triangle
point	isosceles right triangle	edge

Additional Activities

1. Make the Cat, Dog and other MIM animals. Discuss animal sounds.

2. Prepare dioramas showing animals in their natural environments.

3. Read E.B. White's classic, *Charlotte's Web*.

4. Make three *Math in Motion* Pig puppets (glue to popsicle sticks) and the Wolf to dramatize *The Three Little Pigs* (Brothers Grimm). Many children's fables and stories give the wolf a bad name. Describe what's wrong with the way the wolf is portrayed in the story. Retell it. Give the wolf a new personality and the story a new twist.

5. Use analogies to develop auditory association and vocabulary. Read the analogies aloud and emphasize the key words in each analogy.

Mothers and Their Babies

Dog is to **puppy** as cat is to **(kitten)**.   Bear is to **cub** as deer is to **(fawn)**.

Pig is to **piglet** as frog is to **(tadpole)**.   Wolf is to **pup** as whale is to **(calf)**.

Cow is to **calf** as horse is to **(foal)**.

Pig

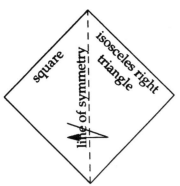

1 Start with a square so it looks like a diamond. Fold the left point over to meet the right point. Unfold.

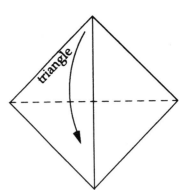

2 Fold the top point down to meet the bottom point.

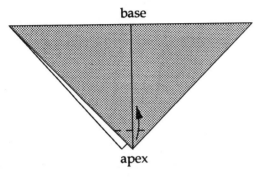

3 Now there are two layers. Fold the top layer up to make a small triangle.

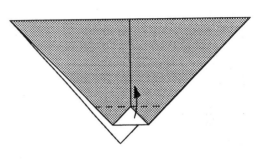

4 Fold the small triangle up again to form the snout.

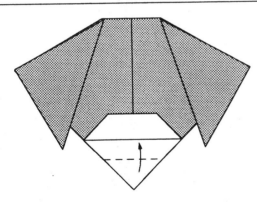

5 Fold the bottom point up and tuck it inside.

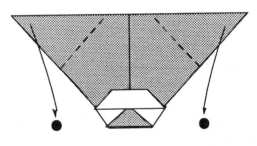

6 Fold the right and left points down to the dots to form ears. These ears will cover part of the face.

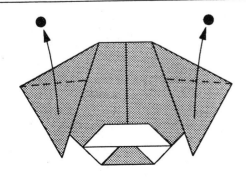

7 Fold the points of the ears up to the dots.

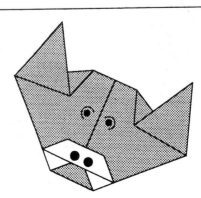

8 Oink! Oink! Draw eyes and nostrils.

Candy Cane

This is a fun holiday model for all ages. Roll the paper tightly around a pencil. Slip the pencil out to shape. Young children may find it tricky to roll the paper.

Strand: Geometry • Vocabulary • Spatial Visualization

Materials: A 6-8-inch square, white side up. Color or draw a pattern on one side of the paper. Tape or glue. (optional)
Alternative: Precut holiday gift wrapping paper into squares.

Concepts and Vocabulary:

square	equal	quadrilateral
letter "L"	vertical	horizontal
opposite	corner	side

Additional Activities:

1. Make a list of all the words that start with the letter "L": love, life, like, learn. Write the words inside Step #3 on the white side of the paper. Brainstorm-- how many words can you think of? Look additional words up in the dictionary. Make this a cooperative activity. Some of the words will appear on the outside of the paper when you roll it.

2. Wrapped in Wishes: Write a message of peace, joy, and hope. Roll it up. Exchange with other classmates or another school.

3. Make several candy canes to decorate holiday packages or trim a tree. 🌲

4. Discuss the multiple meanings of the word cane: sugar • candy • walking aid for the handicapped or injured.

5. Discuss what other cultures use to celebrate holidays or festivals: Mexican piñata, Chinese New Year dragon, Japanese tea ceremony ☕, Jewish dreidle ✡, Irish shamrock ♣.

Candy Cane

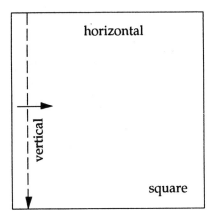

1 Start with a square, white side up. Fold the left vertical side over about 1/2 inch.

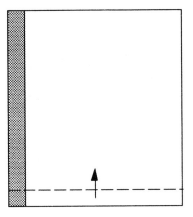

2 Fold the bottom horizontal edge about 1/2 inch up to form the letter "L."

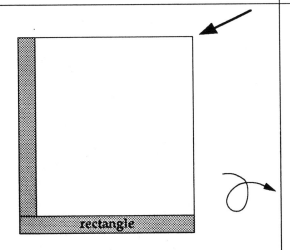

3 Hold the top right corner (on the white side), and turn the paper over. **DON'T LET GO!**

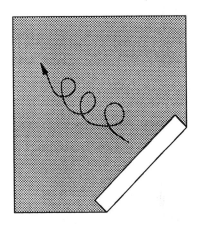

4 Roll the corner you are holding to the opposite corner. **Optional:** Use a pencil to roll the paper and slip it out to shape.

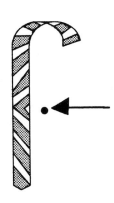

5 Pinch the center point closed. Use glue or tape as needed to hold it in place. Press the top half flat. Curl it over to form a hook.

6 Happy Holidays!

Cup

This practical model is FUNctional!

Strand: Geometry • Spatial Sense

Material: Square, white side up.

Concepts and Vocabulary:

square	quadrilateral	triangle
side	scalene triangle	horizontal
diagonal	line of symmetry	triangle
edge	isosceles right triangle	bottom
layer	trapezoid	pocket (opening)

Additional Activities:

1. Discuss what you could put inside your cup: healthy snacks, fruit, popcorn, peanuts, raisins.

2. Will the cup hold liquid? Test over a sink or plastic container. Experiment using different paper materials: brown paper, lunch, and shopping bags, typing, construction, computer, and notebook paper.

3. Name other items that hold liquid: glass, bowl, bucket, bottle, pot, jar.

4. Save a bug * in your cup and set it free. Read the delightful children's story, *I Was Walking Down the Road* by Sarah E. Barchas (K-2).

5. Make a life-size model out of a 20-inch square (adjust the dimensions) to fit your head. Decorate.

Cup

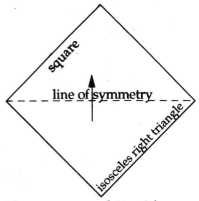

1 Start with a square, white side up. Fold in half along the dotted line.

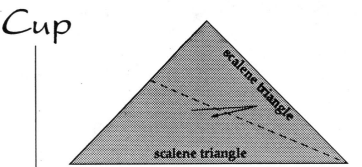

2 Fold the right edge of the top layer to the bottom edge. Unfold.

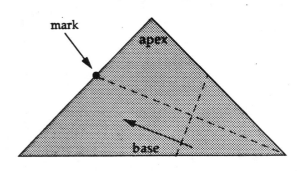

3 Fold the bottom right corner along the dotted line to the **mark** on the opposite side. Crease sharply.

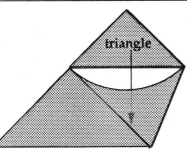

4 See the pocket in the flap you have just made? Fold the top (front) triangle above the pocket downward and slide the triangle into the pocket of the cup as far as it will go.

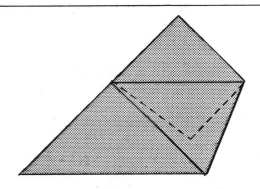

5 Flap is now locked into place. Turn over.

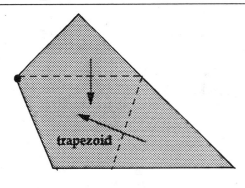

6 Repeat steps #3 and #4.

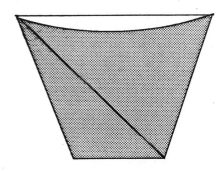

7 Finished cup!

8 Made of paper (newspaper) about 23 inches square, the cup becomes a hat!

Picture Frame

This model makes a great gift! It requires accuracy in folding.

Strand: Geometry • Spatial Sense • Patterns

Materials: A 6-inch or larger square, colored on one side.

Hint: A 6-inch square fits a 3-inch picture. Try a rectangle.

Concepts and Vocabulary:

square	quadrilateral
equal	side
halves	quarters
triangle	right triangle

Additional Activities:

1. Unfold the picture frame and explore paper patterns. Discover smaller squares ❑ within larger ❑ squares. Find triangles within triangles. Trace the outline of the shapes with your finger or pencil. How many squares can you find? How many triangles? Number each one. Color squares blue. Color triangles red. Create different colored patterns. Fold frame again.

2. Recycle! Create-a-frame. Use gift wrapping paper, magazines, old calendars or travel brochures precut into squares (see *Paper Resources* for more ideas). Make frames at home from recycled materials. Display.

3. Draw a picture🌷inside the frame as a gift for Mother's and Father's Day, Valentine's Day, birthdays, celebrations or other special occasions.

4. Discuss different kinds of frames (picture, door, window). 🏠

5. Insert student baby ☺ photos and display in class. Have fun guessing who's who. Number the frames. Write the child's name and number on a separate sheet. Compare your answers.

Picture Frame

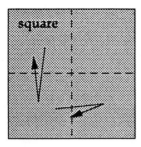

1 Start with a square, colored side up. Fold the bottom edge up to the top. Unfold. Fold the left side to the right side. Unfold.

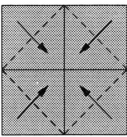

perpendicular lines

2 Fold each corner to the midpoint.

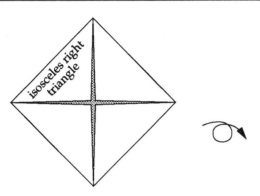

3 It looks like this. Turn over.

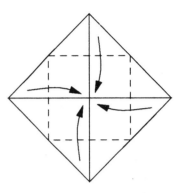

4 Fold each corner to the midpoint again.

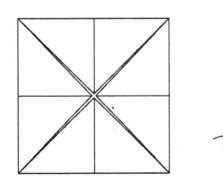

5 Now it looks like this. Turn over again.

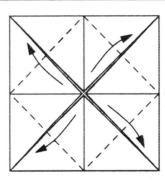

6 Starting at the midpoint, fold each inside corner to the outside corner, forming small triangles.

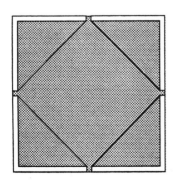

7 Turn the picture frame over.

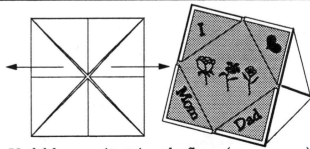

8 Unfold opposite triangle flaps (see arrows) so that they are perpendicular to the side edges of the frame, (pointing up). The frame will lean slightly backwards as it rests on the slanted edges of the flaps.

How to Make an Isosceles Right Triangle from a Square

An isosceles right triangle has two sides the same length.
A right trianlge has one square corner.
An isosceles right triangle has both.
Follow steps #1-3 to make an isosceles right triangle.

1 Fold the square on the diagonal. Unfold.

2 Cut on the diagonal line.

3 Two isosceles right triangles.

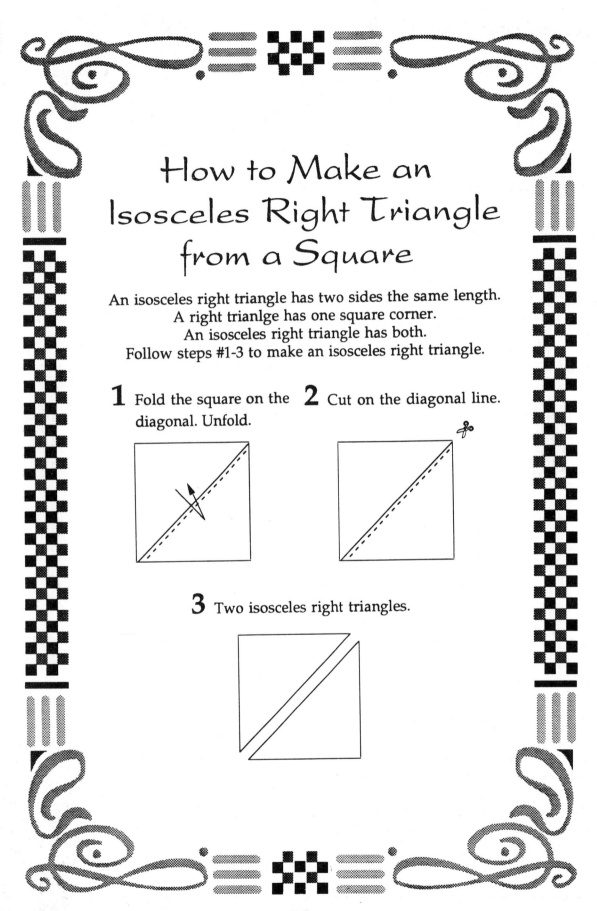

Models Made from Triangles

This model is ideal for younger children. It only has a few steps and is easy to teach.

Strand: Geometry • Spatial Sense

Materials: Triangle. *Cut a square on the diagonal to form 2 triangles.* Instruct students to "pair share," a cooperative term used when students work cooperatively toward a common goal. Allow time to explore. 1) Ask students to find a square shape by matching their triangle with another student. Discover that 2 isosceles right triangles = 1 square. 2) Make a larger triangle. 3) Place one triangle on top of the other triangle to form a six-pointed star. What other shapes can you find?

Concepts and Vocabulary:

triangle	isosceles right triangle	right
apex (top)	right angle	left
base (bottom)	side	up
congruent	edge	down

Additional Activities:

1. Decorate the classroom by hanging up origami dogs on a clothesline. Write a poem on the back of the dog or attach it to a short story.

2. Celebrate National Pet Week (the first week in May).

3. Discuss different breeds of dogs (Collie, Greyhound, Dalmatian). Write a report about your favorite kind of dog. Display on a bulletin.

4. Glue popsicle sticks on the back of the dog and have a puppet show. Read Steven Kellogg's series on *Pinkerton.* (K-3) or make up a play.

Dog

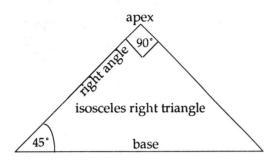

1 Start with a triangle, white side up.

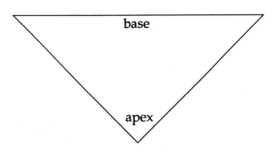

2 Put the triangle on the table so the apex is pointing down.

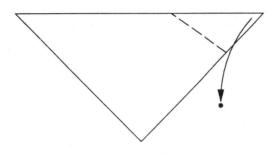

3 Fold one side down to make an ear.

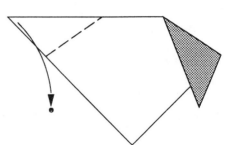

4 Repeat on the other side.

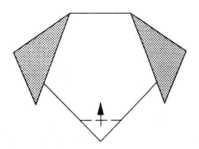

5 Fold the bottom point up to make a small triangle to form the mouth.

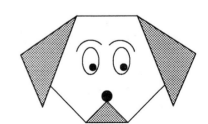

6 Bow-wow! Draw the dog's face. You have made a dog with floppy ears!

How to Fold the Dog

1. Start with a triangle shape. Discuss the characteristics of a triangle. Have students write their answers on the triangle.

    *What is the top part of the **triangle**?*   **Apex.**

    What is the bottom part of the triangle?   **Base.**

    How many sides does a triangle have?   Three.
    Points? Angles?   Three. Three.

    *Are the sides of the triangle the   Yes, two **sides** are exactly the same
    same length?*   length (**congruent**).

    Estimate the length of each side and measure with a ruler. Use standard and metric. How close did you come? Answers will vary according to the size of your triangle.

    What kind of triangle is it?   **Isosceles right triangle.**

    What is an isosceles right triangle?   A triangle that has two congruent
    sides and one **right angle.**

    What is a right angle?   An angle that forms a square corner
    and measures 90°.

    Trace the right angle. Draw a right angle symbol. See the *Dog* diagram, step #1.

    What do the other angles measure?   The other angles measure 45°.

    What is the sum of the angles?   The sum of the angles of a triangle
    is 180°. Check your answers with a
    protractor.

2. Place the triangle on the table so the apex or top is pointing down.

3. Fold the **right** side **down** to form an ear, as shown.

4. Repeat on the **left** side.

5. Fold the bottom point **up** into the shape of a small triangle to form a mouth.

6. Draw the dog's face. Ichi, ni, san, (l, 2, 3) look how much fun math can be!!!

MATH WORD SEARCH

Directions: Find the following words. L👀k vertical (up and down) and horizontal (across).

ANGLE
GEOMETRY
MATH
ORIGAMI
PARALLEL

PERPENDICULAR
RECTANGLE
SQUARE
SYMMETRY
TRIANGLE

K	U	A	R	E	T	R	A	P	H	P	R
T	O	R	I	G	A	M	I	E	U	A	I
U	M	H	R	E	T	C	T	R	L	R	A
L	A	K	G	O	Q	U	A	P	A	A	N
A	T	Z	T	M	F	H	C	E	R	L	G
N	H	A	R	E	C	T	A	N	G	L	E
F	E	N	I	T	T	U	A	D	J	E	H
Q	M	G	A	R	H	L	S	I	J	L	H
L	A	L	N	Y	G	N	Y	C	K	O	E
P	T	X	G	D	Y	N	M	U	T	A	M
X	I	I	L	S	F	K	M	L	U	N	A
E	C	A	E	R	E	C	E	A	L	G	I
E	S	Q	U	A	R	E	T	R	A	L	O
O	T	A	N	U	N	I	R	E	N	E	K
W	G	A	M	I	M	P	Y	A	F	U	N

Try-Angles

The right angle to solve a problem is the try-angle.

Explore different kinds of triangles.
Trace the triangles. Measure the angles
with a protractor and draw another one.

1. Isosceles triangle - a triangle that has
at least two congruent (same) sides.
(See *How to Make an Isosceles Right
Triangle from a Square*)

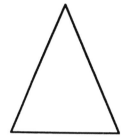

2. Right triangle - a triangle that has
one right angle.

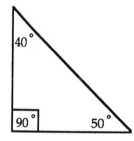

3. Scalene triangle - a triangle that has
no congruent sides.

4. Equilateral triangle - a triangle that has
three sides of equal length. (See *How to
Make an Equilateral Triangle from a Rectangle*)

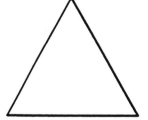

Triangle Tower

Circle the name of the triangle.
scalene   right   isosceles   equilateral
How many triangles can you find?
Color the triangles.

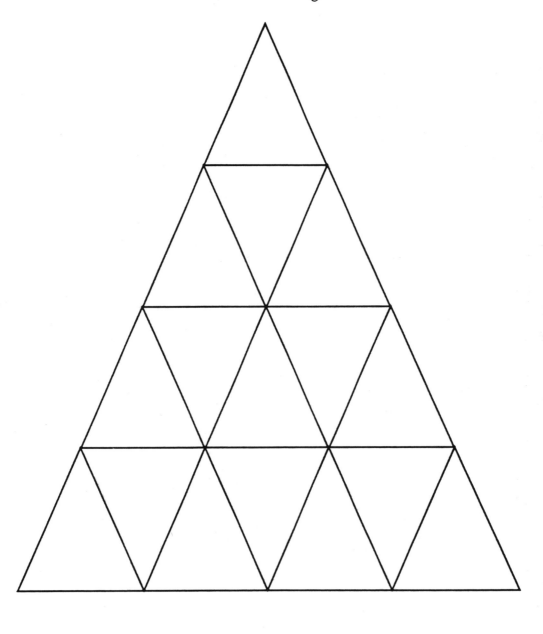

Answer_____triangles

Answer: 27
isosceles triangle

How to Make an Equilateral Triangle from a Rectangle

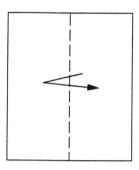

1 Start with an 8.5" x 11" rectangle. Fold in half lengthwise. Unfold.

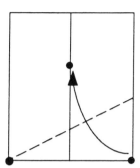

2 Fold from bottom right corner up to center crease line. Make sure the line also intersects (crosses) the bottom left corner.

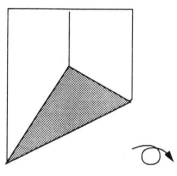

3 Turn over.

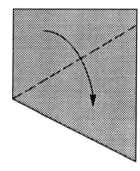

4 Fold the top down to lie flush with the layer underneath.

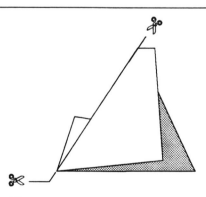

5 Cut off flaps front and back.

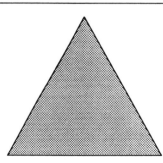

6 **Wow!** An equilateral triangle. Invent an origami model.

Cat

This model is easy for younger children and there are very few steps.

Strand: Geometry • Spatial Sense

Materials: Triangle

Hint: Cut a square on the diagonal to form two triangles. "Pair Share" (See Material guidelines for *Dog).*

Concepts and Vocabulary:

triangle	isosceles right triangle	pentagon
apex (top)	base (bottom)	congruent (same)
side	up	down
right	left	point

Additional Activities:

1. Read and dramatize *The Three Little Kittens.* or Dr. Seuss, *Cat in the Hat Books.* Attach popsicle sticks to make puppets.

2. Make other *Math in Motion* animals and discuss their differences: size, what they eat, where they live, and what sounds they make.

3. Make an animal mobile (see *How to Make an Origami Mobile*).

4. Halloween: cards, place mats, centerpieces, decorate windows.

5. Discuss different breeds of cats (Burmese, Persian, Siamese). Write a report about your favorite kind of cat. Attach the origami cat to the report. Display on a bulletin board.

Cat

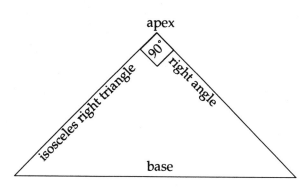

apex

90°

isosceles right triangle

right angle

base

1 Begin with a triangle, white side up.

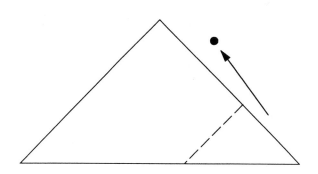

2 Fold one point up to the dot to make an ear.

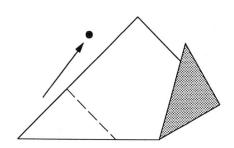

3 Repeat with the other point.

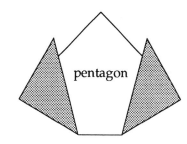

pentagon

4 Now it looks like a tulip.

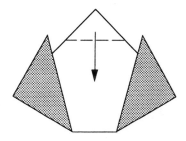

5 Fold the top point down to make another triangle.

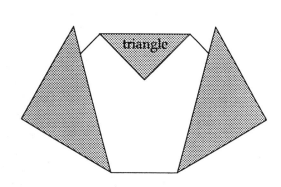

triangle

6 It looks like this.

7 Turn over. Meow! Draw a face and whiskers.

Sailboat

Ship ahoy mates! This action model is suitable for kids of all ages.

Strand: Geometry • Spatial Sense • Measurement

Materials: Begin with a triangle, white side up.

Hint: Cut a square on the diagonal to form 2 triangles.

Concepts and Vocabulary:

triangle	right triangle
point	angle
apex	base
side	halfway

Additional Activities:

1. Gently blow the sailboat across your desk. Measure the distance your boat travels before it capsizes. Make it a cooperative activity. Record the outcome and tally the best score out of five. Graph the results.

2. Sail ahead with *Math in Motion*. Write your name on the boat sails and use as name cards, decorate a bulletin board or glue onto a card.

3. For Columbus Day, make three boats representing the Niña, Pinta and Santa Maria.

4. Thanksgiving: Discuss how the Pilgrims traveled to the New World. Fold a boat to represent the Mayflower. Write a story about it. Attach the ship.

5. Comparatives. Make three *Math in Motion* sailboats of different sizes. Teach the concept of big, bigger, biggest.

Sailboat

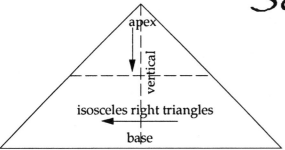

1 Begin with a triangle, white side up. Put the triangle on the table with the longest side toward you (base). Fold the triangle in half along the vertical dotted line. Unfold. Fold the top point (apex) down to the bottom edge (base) of the triangle (see step #2).

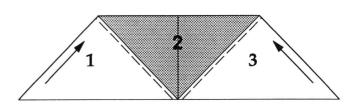

2 Fold triangle 1 up along the dotted line. Now it covers part of the center of triangle 2. Repeat with triangle 3.

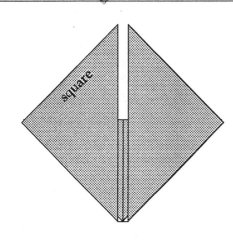

3 Now the two side triangles cover most of the center triangle.

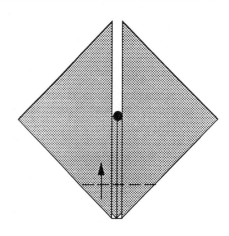

4 Fold the bottom point halfway up to form a small triangle.

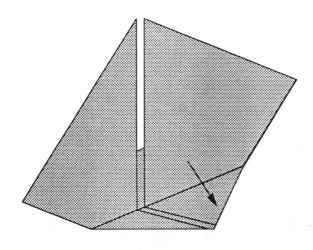

5 Pull the small triangle back (toward you) to make a stand.

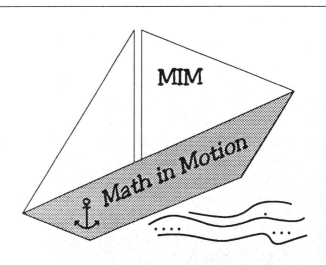

6 Turn it around to discover a sailboat. Sail ahead with *Math in Motion!*

Sailboat ▲ Tulip ▲ Dog

These diagrams illustrate how some shapes can be transformed into different models. Fold the sailboat base into a tulip and a dog. Challenge students to study the patterns in other diagrams and have fun creating original models.

## Sailboat	## Tulip	## Dog
 **1** Fold along vertical dotted line. Unfold. Fold in half along horizontal dotted line.	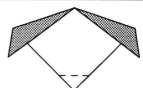 **1** Unfold the sailboat. Study the patterns on the paper. Fold each bottom corner up along the dotted line.	 **1** Turn the tulip upside down. Fold the bottom point up along the dotted line.
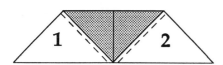 **2** Fold triangle 1 up along the diagonal dotted line. Repeat with triangle 2.	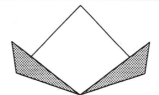 **2** Now you have a tulip! Color the tulip.	 **2** Now you have a dog! Draw the dog's face.

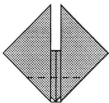

3 Fold up along the dotted line to make a stand for the sailboat.

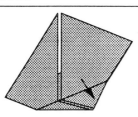

4 Pull the small triangle back (toward you) to make a stand.

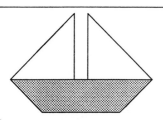

5 Turn over to see your finished sailboat!

I

♥

Math

in

Motion!

Part VI

Cultural
&
Educational
Enrichment

*A*nyone who says you can't see a thought simply doesn't know art.

Wynetka Ann Reynolds

Math in Motion

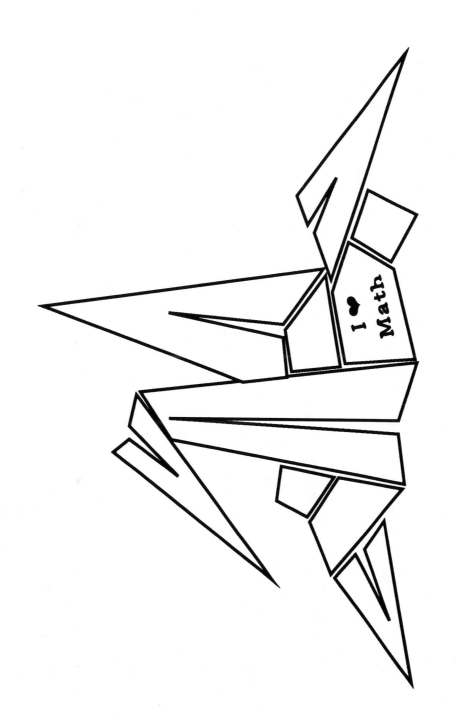

The crane is a symbol of good luck, long life and peace. Color the crane for a bright ☼ and happy future.

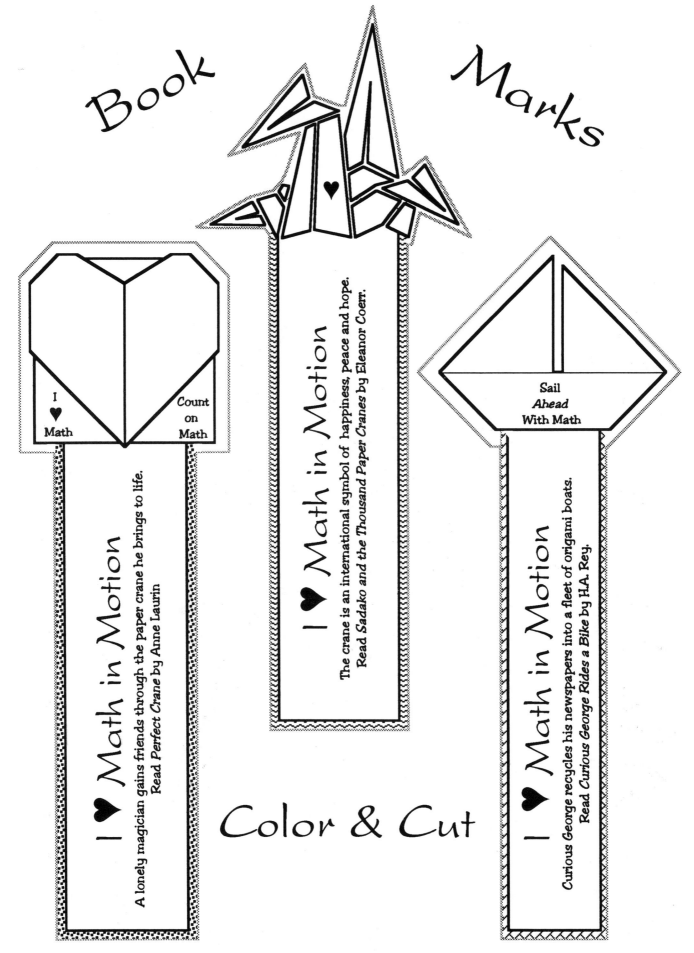

Book Marks

Color & Cut

I ♥ Math in Motion

A lonely magician gains friends through the paper crane he brings to life.
Read Perfect Crane by Anne Laurin

I
♥
Math

Count
on
Math

I ♥ Math in Motion

The crane is an international symbol of happiness, peace and hope.
Read Sadako and the Thousand Paper Cranes by Eleanor Coerr.

I ♥ Math in Motion

Curious George recycles his newspapers into a fleet of origami boats.
Read Curious George Rides a Bike by H.A. Rey.

Sail
Ahead
With Math

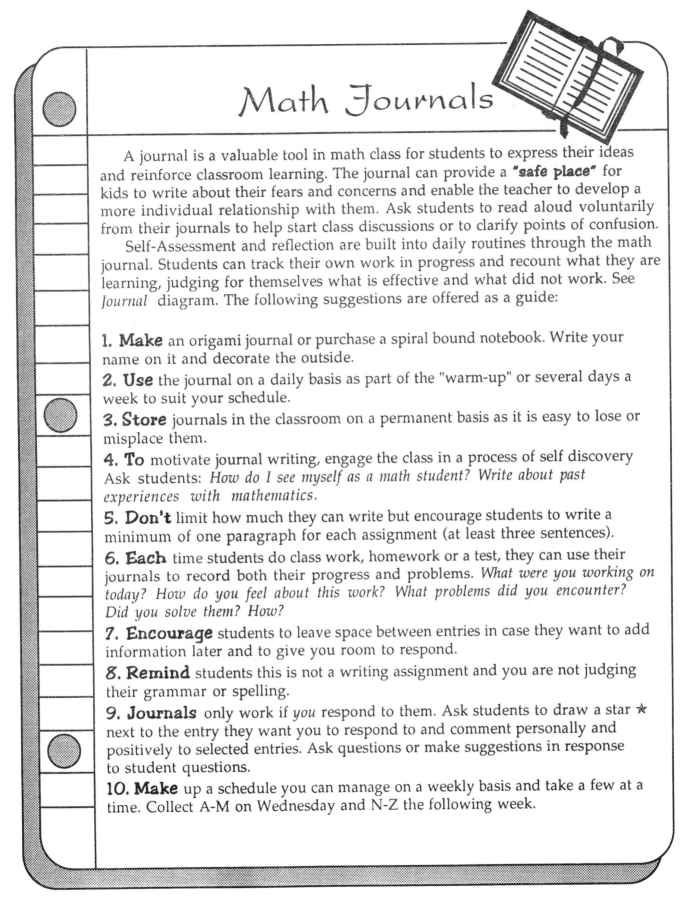

Math Journals

A journal is a valuable tool in math class for students to express their ideas and reinforce classroom learning. The journal can provide a **"safe place"** for kids to write about their fears and concerns and enable the teacher to develop a more individual relationship with them. Ask students to read aloud voluntarily from their journals to help start class discussions or to clarify points of confusion.

Self-Assessment and reflection are built into daily routines through the math journal. Students can track their own work in progress and recount what they are learning, judging for themselves what is effective and what did not work. See *Journal* diagram. The following suggestions are offered as a guide:

1. **Make** an origami journal or purchase a spiral bound notebook. Write your name on it and decorate the outside.

2. **Use** the journal on a daily basis as part of the "warm-up" or several days a week to suit your schedule.

3. **Store** journals in the classroom on a permanent basis as it is easy to lose or misplace them.

4. **To** motivate journal writing, engage the class in a process of self discovery Ask students: *How do I see myself as a math student? Write about past experiences with mathematics.*

5. **Don't** limit how much they can write but encourage students to write a minimum of one paragraph for each assignment (at least three sentences).

6. **Each** time students do class work, homework or a test, they can use their journals to record both their progress and problems. *What were you working on today? How do you feel about this work? What problems did you encounter? Did you solve them? How?*

7. **Encourage** students to leave space between entries in case they want to add information later and to give you room to respond.

8. **Remind** students this is not a writing assignment and you are not judging their grammar or spelling.

9. **Journals** only work if *you* respond to them. Ask students to draw a star ★ next to the entry they want you to respond to and comment personally and positively to selected entries. Ask questions or make suggestions in response to student questions.

10. **Make** up a schedule you can manage on a weekly basis and take a few at a time. Collect A-M on Wednesday and N-Z the following week.

Pearls of Wisdom

A quotation paints a portrait of ideas and thoughts. The following are some of my favorite quotations. Write, "Thought for the Week," on one side of the chalkboard and select an inspiring quotation, positive affirmation or word. Encourage students to bring in their favorite quotes, short poems or lyrics. At the end of the week, ask students to reflect on their thoughts in their origami journals (see *Journal* diagram). Underline a word from the phrase that captures its meaning. Draw a picture to describe the word. Share your responses with the class or another student.

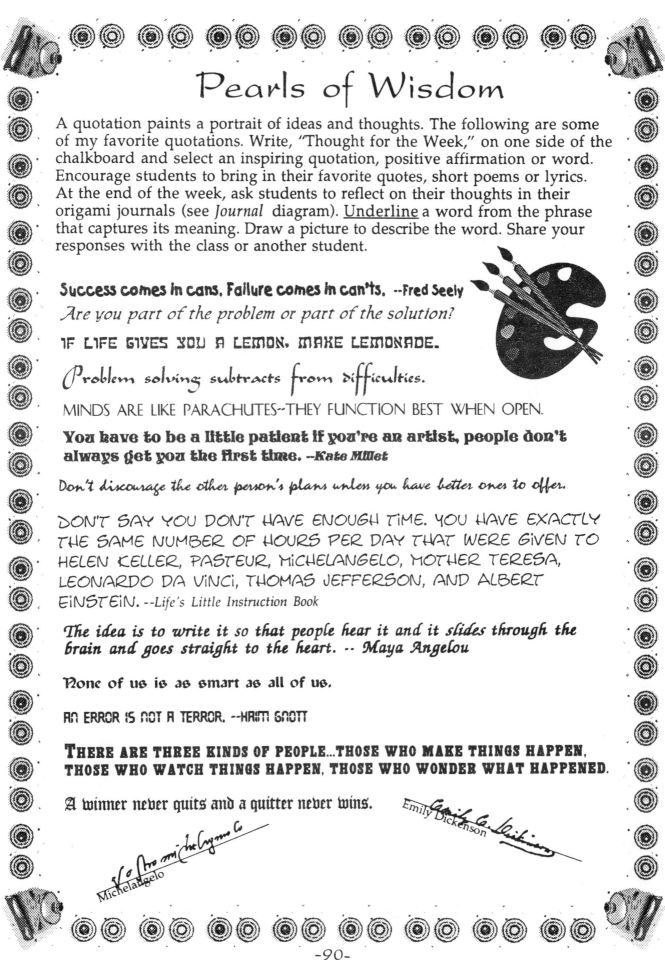

Success comes in cans. Failure comes in can'ts. --Fred Seely

Are you part of the problem or part of the solution?

IF LIFE GIVES YOU A LEMON, MAKE LEMONADE.

Problem solving subtracts from difficulties.

MINDS ARE LIKE PARACHUTES--THEY FUNCTION BEST WHEN OPEN.

You have to be a little patient if you're an artist, people don't always get you the first time. --*Kate Millet*

Don't discourage the other person's plans unless you have better ones to offer.

DON'T SAY YOU DON'T HAVE ENOUGH TIME. YOU HAVE EXACTLY THE SAME NUMBER OF HOURS PER DAY THAT WERE GIVEN TO HELEN KELLER, PASTEUR, MICHELANGELO, MOTHER TERESA, LEONARDO DA VINCI, THOMAS JEFFERSON, AND ALBERT EINSTEIN. --*Life's Little Instruction Book*

The idea is to write it so that people hear it and it slides through the brain and goes straight to the heart. -- *Maya Angelou*

None of us is as smart as all of us.

AN ERROR IS NOT A TERROR. --HAIM GNOTT

THERE ARE THREE KINDS OF PEOPLE...THOSE WHO MAKE THINGS HAPPEN, THOSE WHO WATCH THINGS HAPPEN, THOSE WHO WONDER WHAT HAPPENED.

A winner never quits and a quitter never wins.   Emily Dickenson

Michelangelo

I'm a Japanese Fan

The fan is a symbol of good luck.
It represents the unfolding future.
Write something new that you have learned
about today inside each section of the fan.
Color the fan bright ☼ colors.

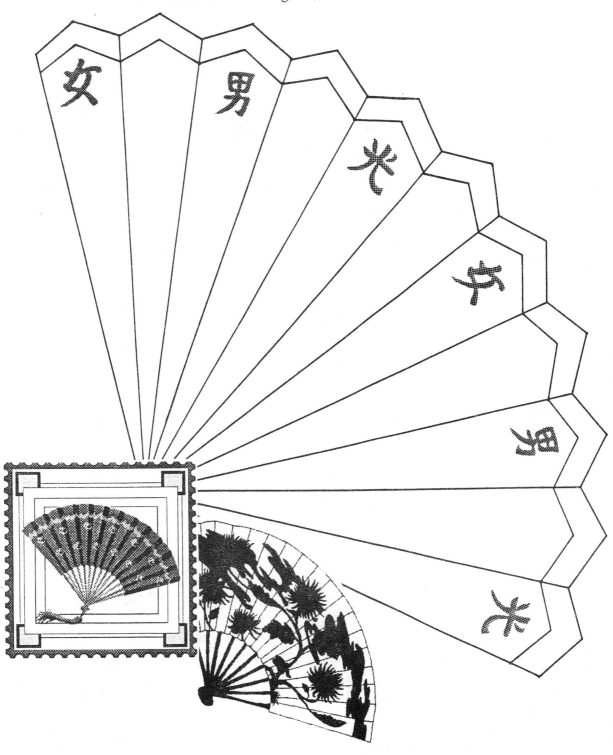

Dot to Dot ∴

Japan is famous for dancers who wear elaborate costumes.
This type of special entertainment has been popular for many years.
Connect the dots in order and color the dancer.

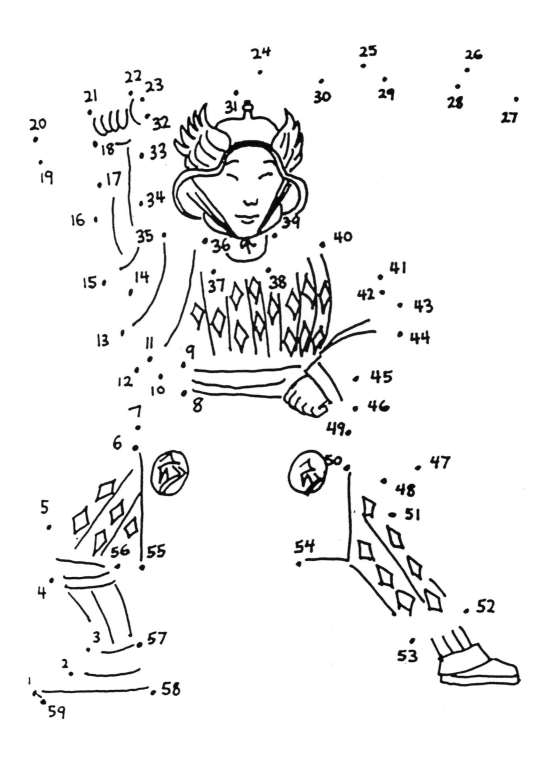

Maze Craze

Help the crane find the bonsai tree.
The bonsai tree is a Japanese miniature tree.
The crane is an international symbol of
peace, happiness and good luck.

Have Fun With Haiku

Haiku (hai-ku), is a Japanese poem about feelings and nature. It comes from two Japanese words meaning "play" and "poem." Each poem has three lines and contains 17 syllables. **The first and third lines have five syllables each and the second line has seven syllables.** Count the syllables in each line. These haiku poems were written by children.

Flowers are blooming (5)
birds are singing in the trees (7)
spring is everywhere. (5)
         -- Jason

The graceful crane flies
high above the mountain tops
show me how to soar.
         – Erica

Snow flakes in the sky
drift slowly to the wet ground
one cold winter day.
         -- Seth

Close your eyes. Think about nature. Write a Japanese haiku poem and illustrate it.

_____

_____

_____

One Fish, Two Fish, No Fish?

You need
• A group of kids • Fishing rods (sticks with a string and magnet tied to the end) • Lots of pieces of paper measuring 2" by 3.5" (old business cards or used wrapping paper work great)

The game
• Fold 25 fish and put a paperclip on each one • Have 1 kid start fishing, catching fish with the magnet • Meanwhile have 2 kids fold more fish • Keep adding more and more fishermen

The goal
• What's a sustainable number of fishermen for your pond? What happens when you have more than that number? Find the right balance between fish and fishermen, and you've achieved sustainable fishing! Discuss how you think this game compares with what happens in the real world.

Something's fishy about these fish!

How to make the fish
a) Cut out the rectangle (or use old business cards)
b) Fold corners 1,2 and 3 forward
c) Fold corner 4 behind

Cut out the diagram and make your own fish!

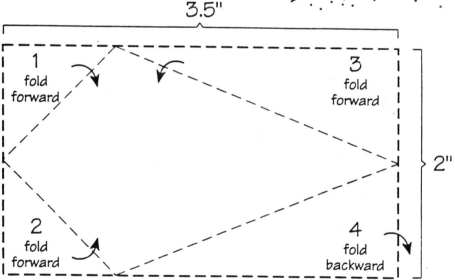

3.5"

| 1 fold forward | 3 fold forward |
| 2 fold forward | 4 fold backward |

2"

What is Sustainable Living?
It means finding a way of life that can continue for years without harming the environment. For farming, it means growing food without using a lot of water or harmful pesticides. In transportation, it means using mass transit like buses, trains or walking, biking or even using a solar powered car.

Most of today's environmental problems were created by people not living in a sustainable way. For example: Just 10 years ago very few U.S. households recycled. Landfills were filling up fast. Today, three times as many households recycle. And many people are finding ways to produce less waste by reducing packaging and buying reusable products. Learn more ways to protect the Earth. Read *50 Simple Things Kids Can Do To Save the Earth* by The Earth Works Group.

Can You Speak Japanese?

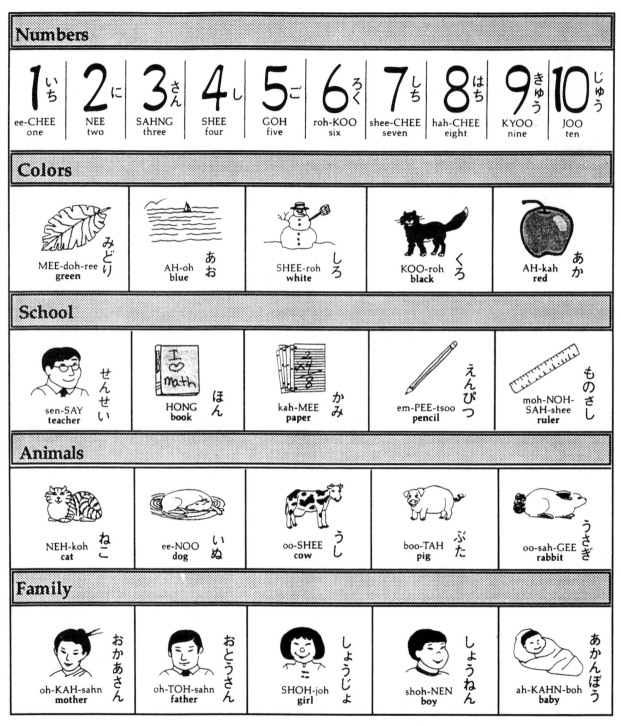

Numbers

1 いち	2 に	3 さん	4 し	5 ご	6 ろく	7 しち	8 はち	9 きゅう	10 じゅう
ee-CHEE one	NEE two	SAHNG three	SHEE four	GOH five	roh-KOO six	shee-CHEE seven	hah-CHEE eight	KYOO nine	JOO ten

Colors

みどり	あお	しろ	くろ	あか
MEE-doh-ree **green**	AH-oh **blue**	SHEE-roh **white**	KOO-roh **black**	AH-kah **red**

School

せんせい	ほん	かみ	えんぴつ	ものさし
sen-SAY **teacher**	HONG **book**	kah-MEE **paper**	em-PEE-tsoo **pencil**	moh-NOH-SAH-shee **ruler**

Animals

ねこ	いぬ	うし	ぶた	うさぎ
NEH-koh **cat**	ee-NOO **dog**	oo-SHEE **cow**	boo-TAH **pig**	oo-sah-GEE **rabbit**

Family

おかあさん	おとうさん	しょうじょ	しょうねん	あかんぼう
oh-KAH-sahn **mother**	oh-TOH-sahn **father**	SHOH-joh **girl**	shoh-NEN **boy**	ah-KAHN-boh **baby**

The words on this page are written in Hiragana, a simple system of sounds used by Japanese children who are learning to read and write. By the time they finish high school they will learn over 2,000 characters.

Find the picture, how Japanese children might write the word, how it is pronounced in Japanese and the English word.

Writing Japanese Numbers

English	Japanese	Sound	Written
one	ichi	ee-che	一
two	nik	nee	二
three	san	san	三
four	shi	she	四
five	go	go	五
six	roku	row-coo	六
seven	shichi	she-che	七
eight	hachi	ha-che	八
nine	ku	coo	九
ten	ju	ju	十
zero	zero	zee-row	〇

Write your answers using Japanese words and numbers.

Example: 10 + 7 = 17   17 = ju + shichi = ju shichi   十七

1. What is your age? _____

2. How many brothers and sisters do you have?_____

3. How many days in a week? _____

4. Write your telephone number. _____

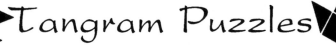

Tangram Puzzles

A tangram is an ancient Chinese puzzle.
The Chinese made tangram patterns to
represent cats, boats and other objects.
The seven geometrical shapes:

one **square**

one **parallelogram**

two small **triangles**

one medium **triangle**

and two large **triangles**

fit together to make a square.
Label each shape and follow the directions.

1. Color the seven geometrical parts.

2. Cut out the shapes.

3. Make a square using all seven pieces.

4. Create some of the patterns.

5. Make your own designs.

6. Read *Grandfather Tang's Story*.

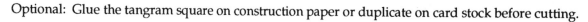

Optional: Glue the tangram square on construction paper or duplicate on card stock before cutting.

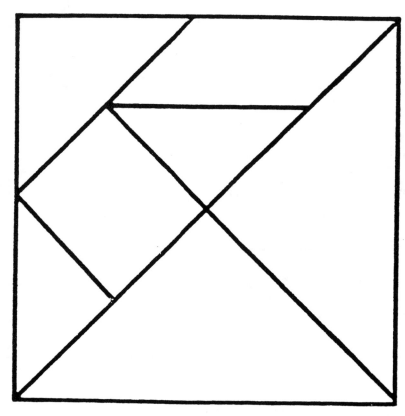

Fortune Cookies

Make up math fortunes to insert in the cookies. Have students make up their own math quotes or reinforce math vocabulary and concepts. To make fortunes, cut paper into strips about 2 inches long and 3/4 inches wide. Type or write a fortune on each side. Ask a parent volunteer to make the cookies and insert the fortunes. Here are some examples:

Count on math.	Math is FUNctional.
I ♥ math.	Math makes a difference.
Math adds up.	It's the thought that counts.
Math Power for All.	Math teachers count a lot.

Recipe: 1 cup margarine, softened
1/2 cup sugar (caution: sugar alternatives may not
1 egg   yield the same results)
2-1/2 teaspoons vanilla extract
3-1/4 cups flour
1/2 teaspoon baking powder

1. Mix together margarine, sugar and egg until smooth. Then add other ingredients. Mix everything together to form a ball of dough.

2. Lightly flour a wooden board or flat surface. With a rolling pin, roll half of the dough very thin. Use a circle-shaped cookie cutter or the top of a large glass about 2-1/2 inches wide to cut circles in dough.

3. Put a fortune in each circle, off to one side. Fold the circle in half and then in half again. Pinch to close.

4. Preheat the oven to 425°.

5. Reroll cut scraps of dough and make cookies from them. Then roll and make cookies from the other half of the dough.

6. Bake cookies about 10 minutes or until they are lightly browned.

Makes 25 cookies.

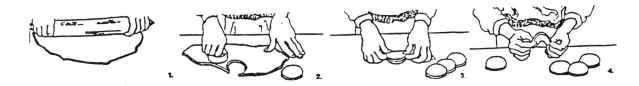

A Thousand Cranes of Origami

"I will write 'peace' on your wings and you will fly all over the world."

--*Sadako Sasaki*

There is an old belief in Japan that a crane can live a thousand years; and that if you fold 1,000 paper cranes you will live a long life and they will keep you well.

Twelve year old Sadako Sasaki made 644 paper cranes before she died of leukemia, ten years after the atomic bomb fell on Hiroshima.

Her friends and classmates collected 7,000,000 yen ($20,000) to build a monument to Sadako and other child victims of the bomb.

Over the years, Sadako's life and death have become well known. The paper crane has become an international symbol of peace. Read *Sadako and the Thousand Paper Cranes* by Eleanor Coerr.

Today, children from all over the world send paper cranes to decorate Sadako's monument, a statue of a young girl, standing atop a mountain, holding a golden crane in her outstretched hands. At the base of the statue, it reads:

"This is our cry, this is our prayer: peace in the world."

The Thousand Crane Club invites children to participate in folding paper cranes to promote world peace. The crane is a challenging model and recommended for ages 8 and older. Informed Democracy offers videos based on the story *Sadako and the Thousand Paper Cranes* and *How to Fold a Paper Crane* (see *Videos for Paper Folders*). Send your cranes to:

Thousand Crane Club
Hiroshima International School
3-49-1, Kurakake, Asa Kita-ku
Hiroshima 739-17, Japan

How to Make an Origami Mobile

A mobile is a hanging ornament of parts that move.
Origami makes a great mobile because it is lightweight and moves easily.

Materials: Several origami models, a needle, invisible thread, glue, thin soft wire, and wire cutters. These items can be purchased in an arts and crafts or a fabric store.

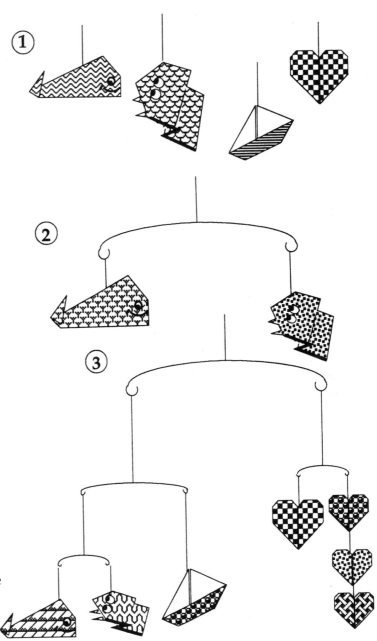

First, thread all your models. Vary the length of the thread to arrange the way you want each one to hang. (Fig.1)

Cut a piece of wire and tie a model to each end. Make a loop at the end of the wire to keep the thread from slipping off. Glue the knots in place.

Tie a thread to the middle of the wire and slide it back and forth to balance the models. Glue the knot to the wire. (Fig. 2)

Tie the pair of models to one end of a longer wire. Place one model or another pair at the other end. Tie a thread to the wire and balance. (Fig. 3)

Continue to work from the bottom upward and use longer wires to hang all your models. Make the wires long enough so that none of the models touch each other as they move around in circles. Finally, balance a thread to hang up the mobile. An origami mobile of bright colors can decorate a room or make a colorful gift for a new baby or a friend!

Aa Bb Cc Dd Ee Ff Gg Hh Ii Jj Kk Ll Mm Nn Oo Pp Qq Rr Ss Tt Uu Vv Ww Xx Yy Zz

Mathematics

How many words can you find in mathematics?
Each word should have at least two or more letters.
You can use the same letter more than once. Example: meet.
Write three sentences using as many of the words as you can.
Circle all the words you use in each sentence.

math
team

Math Word Scramble

The following are words you might hear in a math class.
Unscramble the letters and write the words on the line.

1. mtgoyeer_____

2. strenitec_____

3. ymsetmry_____

4. gnale_____

5. qusera_____

6. ncogunter_____

7. cterglean_____

8. irgletna_____

9. arelpall_____

10. dupericpnerla_____

congruent   intersect
angle   symmetry   geometry   triangle
parallel   square   rectangle   perpendicular

Draw a Diagram

The national mathematics standards have identified
the *appreciation* and *enjoyment* of mathematics
as one of the national goals for mathematics education.
" ...Mathematically powerful students think and communicate
drawing mathematical ideas and using
mathematical tools and techniques."

Mathematical power has four dimensions: thinking, communication, ideas and techniques. Drawing a diagram challenges students to organize information, make connections, design, test, verify and reason. Diagram drawing supports national goals for purposeful, enjoyable and active learning.

Directions:

1. Examine and discuss diagrams for an origami model. Study models in origami books or use sample diagrams from *Paper Folding Projects*.
2. Ask students to draw a diagram that represents a model they know how to fold or invent one.
3. Invent a product that will bring world peace.
4. Use symbols to diagram your model (see *Symbols*). Draw other symbols as needed. Include a key.

Students exchange diagrams and fold each others model. Plan time for students to analyze their results with the designer of the model. Encourage students to justify their thinking. Assessment is in the PROOF!

Extension: Ask the class to draw the *same* diagram of a model they know how to fold and compare them. Display on a bulletin board. Students learn there can be *more than one* solution to the same problem.

Part VII

Resources

*W*hat we want is to see the child in pursuit of knowledge, and not the knowledge in pursuit of the child.

George Bernard Shaw

What To Do With Origami

Origami offers *many* opportunities for educational and creative expression. Experiment with different sizes, shapes and colors. Here are a few ideas. Can you think of more?

Decorate greeting cards, note paper and packages.

Make party decorations: invitations, cups, hats, place cards.

Send a message of cheer to a friend; show you care.

Prepare a presentation or book report with models.

Make a friend--teach someone origami.

Make scenes to illustrate a story or a lesson.

Make pieces for a game.

Decorate the holidays; make ornaments for a tree, origami hearts for Valentine's Day, boats for Columbus Day, baskets for Easter, flowers for Spring, whales or other endangered animals for Earth Day.

Pack a model inside a lunch bag with a greeting.

Make finger puppets and create a play or dramatize a story.

Frame your favorite photograph or picture.

Build a fleet of boats, a village, or farm animals.

Catch students doing something right and present them with personalized models of hearts or sailboats.

Make an experience chart emphasizing the sequential steps of a model and invite students in their spare time to fold it. Provide materials.

Children's Origami Exhibit

The Children's Origami Exhibit is an annual event. It is open to all children under the age of 18. The deadline is July 31st. The Exhibit also travels to schools and libraries throughout the country. Send a #10 SASE with two-first class stamps for more information and an application:
Origami by Children
15 West 77th Street
New York, New York 10024

Membership to Origami USA

Certificate of Merit

All Children Welcome

No Experience Necessary

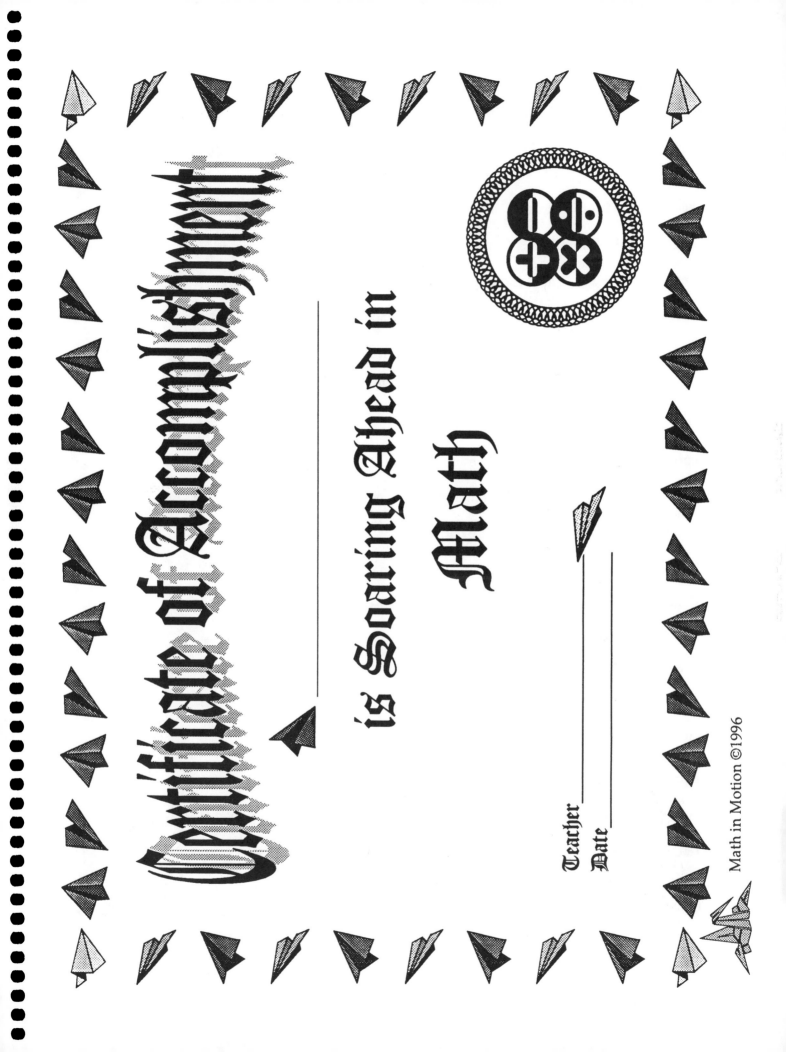

Certificate of Accomplishment

is Soaring Ahead in

Math

Teacher

Date

Math in Motion ©1996

Glossary
English / Spanish
`Inglés / Español`

acute angle/ángulo agudo - an angle that has a measure less than 90°.

angle/ángulo - an angle is formed when two rays have a common endpoint.

answer/respuesta - the solution or response to a problem or a question.

area/área - the number of square units or surface inside a figure.

base/base - a side on which a geometrical figure stands.

bisect/bisecto - a line that divides a geometric figure into two congruent parts.

center/centro - the middle point, place or part.

column/columna - the tall, narrow portion of a figure or object.

congruent/congruente - line segments or figures exactly the same size and shape.

count/contar - the total number or amount.

data/datos - the facts that refer to or describe an object or idea.

denominator/denominador - the bottom number in a fraction. It tells the number of equal parts in the whole unit.

$$\frac{3}{4}$$

degree/grado - a unit for measuring angles and temperature. (°)

diagonal/diagonal - a straight line that crosses in a slanting direction.

endpoint/punto final - a point where a line segment begins or ends.

equal/igual - the same in amount, size, number, or value. (=)

even number/número par - divisible by two, a number that ends in 0, 2, 4, 6 or 8.

fraction/fracción - a number used to name parts of a whole or parts of a group.

geometry/geometría - a branch of mathematics that deals with the relationships between shapes, angles, lines and planes.

halfway/a mitad - midway.

height/altura - a vertical distance usually upwards.

hexagon/hexágono - a polygon with six sides.

horizontal line/línea horizontal - a line parallel to or on level with the horizon.

intersection/intersección - to meet and cross.

intersecting lines/lineas que se cruzan - two or more lines that meet or cross at a common point.

isosceles triangle/triángulo isósceles - a triangle that has at least two congruent (same) sides.

left/izquierda - to one side, opposite of right.

length/longitud - the longest dimension of an object.

line/línea - a straight path that goes forever in both directions.

line of symmetry/línea de simetriá - a line of folding so that the two halves of a figure match.

line segment/segmento lineal - a straight path that has two endpoints.

mathematics/matemática - the science of numbers, measurement, and space.

measure/medir - to find the size or amount.

model/modelo - a design or representation.

numbers/números - symbols used for counting and measuring.

numerator/numerador - the top number in a fraction. $\frac{3}{4}$
It tells how many equal parts are being considered.

obtuse angle/ángulo obtuso - angles that measure greater than 90° less than 180°.

octagon/octágono - a polygon with eight sides.

odd number/número impar - not divisible by two, numbers that end in 1, 3, 5, 7, 9.

opposite/contrario - as different in direction as can be.

parallel lines/líneas paralelas - lines in a plane that never intersect or meet.

parallelogram/líneas paralelogramo - a quadrilateral with 2 pairs of parallel lines.

pattern/modelo - an arrangement of forms, shapes, and colors.

pentagon/pentágono - a polygon with five sides.

perpendicular lines/líneas perpendicular - lines that intersect to form right angles.

plane/plano - a flat surface that continues infinitely in all directions.

point/punto - an exact location in space. (•)

polygon/polígono - a closed figure formed by three or more line segments.

quadrilateral/cuadrilateral - a polygon that has four sides.

ray/rayo - a portion of a line that extends forever in one direction only.

rectangle/rectángulo - a quadrilateral that has four right angles.

right/derecho - to one side.

left	right

right angle/ángulo recto - an angle that forms a square corner and measures 90°.

scalene triangle/triángulo escaleno - a triangle with all sides and angles different.

square/cuadrado - a rectangle with four sides of equal length.

triangle/triángulo - a polygon with three sides; the sum of a triangle equals 180°.

vertex/vértice - the common endpoint of two rays that form an angle.

vertical line/línea vertical - a straight line is perpendicular to a horizontal line in the same place.

volume/volumen - the number of cubic units it takes to fit inside a solid figure.

width/anchura - a distance from side to side.

Numbers / Números

zero	0	cero	sixteen	16	diez y seis
one	1	uno	seventeen	17	diez y siete
two	2	dos	eighteen	18	diez y ocho
three	3	tres	nineteen	19	diez y nueve
four	4	cuatro	twenty	20	veinte
five	5	cinco	twenty-one	21	veintiuno
six	6	seis	thirty	30	treinta
seven	7	siete	thirty-one	31	treinta y uno
eight	8	ocho	forty	40	cuarenta
nine	9	nueve	forty-one	41	cuarenta y uno
ten	10	diez	fifty	50	cincuenta
eleven	11	once	sixty	60	sesenta
twelve	12	doce	seventy	70	setenta
thirteen	13	trece	eighty	80	ochenta
fourteen	14	cuatorce	ninety	90	noventa
fifteen	15	quince	hundred	100	ciento

Suggested Readings • Resources

National Organizations:

National Clearinghouse for U.S.-Japan Studies. Indiana University, 2805 East Tenth Street, Suite 120, Bloomington, Indiana 47408-2698. ☎ 800-266-3815. E-Mail: Japan@Indiana.edu (lesson plans, curriculum guides, journal articles, special reports).

National Council of Teachers of Mathematics (NCTM). 1906 Association Drive, Reston, VA 22091. ☎ 800-235-7566. (request information on Mathematics Education Month in April and other resources).

British Origami Society, 2a The Chestnuts, Countesthorpe, Leicester LE85TL, Great Britain, England. ☎ 0116-277-3870.

Origami USA. 15 West 77th Street, New York, NY 10024. ☎ 212-769-5635. (membership includes newsletter, annual convention, special events, list of regional groups, books and supplies).

The Educational Resources and Information Center--ERIC/Clearinghouse for Science, Mathematics, and Environmental Education. 1929 Kenny Road, Columbus, Ohio 43210-1080. ☎ 800-276-0462. E-mail: ericse@osu.edu (curricula materials, teacher education).

Books for Beginning Paper Folders: *There are many origami books from which to choose. Check your library and bookstores. Add your favorites.*

Kasahara, Kunihiko. *Origami Made Easy.* Tokyo: Japan Publication, 1973.

Lewis, Shari and Oppenheimer, Lillian. *Folding Paper Toys:* Lanham, MD, Scarborough Hse., 1993.

Sakata, Hideaki. *Origami.* Tokyo: Harper & Row, 1984 (color illustrations).

Temko, Florence. *Paper Pandas and Jumping Frogs.* SF: China Books, 1986.

Videos for Paper Folders:

Origami: Square 1. Michael G. LaFosse (instructional series of 4 tapes, beginner to advanced), Exquisite Origami Videotapes, Alexander Brace & Co. Inc., 170 Margin Street, Haverhill, MA 01832-5109. ☎ 800-238-1279.

Sadako and the Thousand Paper Cranes (30 minutes) narrated by Liv Ullmann, 1991 and *How to Fold a Paper Crane* (instructional, 30 minutes) by George Levenson, 1994. Informed Democracy, P. O. Box 67, Santa Cruz, CA, 95063. ☎ 800-827-0949.

Paper Folding Stories:

Kallevig, Christine, Petrell.*Folding Stories--Storytelling and Origami Together as One.* Newburgh, Indiana: Storytime Ink International, 1991.

_____, *Holiday Folding Stories.* Storytime Ink, 1992.

Pellowski, Anne. *Family Storytelling Handbook,* (two paperfolding stories, p.74-84). New York: Macmillian Publishing Company, 1987.

Children's Literature: (multicultural)

Bang, Molly. *The Paper Crane.* New York: William Morrow & Company, Inc. 1985. (a mysterious man pays for his meal with a paper crane that comes alive, K-2).

Okawa, Essei. *The Adventures of the One Inch Boy,* Union City, CA: Heian International, Inc., 1985. (despite his size, a young boy triumphs, K-3).

Carratllo, John and Patty. *Meiko: A Story of Japanese Culture CD-ROM.* produced by Digital Productions Inc., Idyllwild, CA, 1995. Distributed by Broderbund Software ☎ 800-521-6263 (based on a children's story by Leo Politi, comprehensive Teacher's Guide provides classroom activities, 4-6).

Coerr, Eleanor. *Sadako and the Thousand Paper Cranes.* New York: G.P. Putnam's Sons, 1978. (a story about war, courage and peace, 3-6), video also available--see *Videos for Paper Folders.*

Demi. *The Empty Pot.* New York: Henry Holt and Company 1990. (Ping, a young Chinese boy discovers honesty is the best reward, K-2).

Juster, Norton. *The Phantom Tolbboooth.* New York: Random House, 1961. (Milo and his companions travel to Digitopolis, the land of numbers, 4-6), video also available.

Kroll, Virginia. *Pink Paper Swans.* Michigan: Wm. B. Eerdman, 1994. (a young African American girl and a Japanese woman find friendship through paper folding, instructions included, 3-6).

Laurin, Anne. *Perfect Crane.* New York: Harper & Row, 1981. (a lonely magician gains friends through a paper crane he brings to life, 2-4).

Matsutani, Miyoko, *The Crane Maiden.* NY: Parents Magazine Press, 1968. (Japanese folktale, 3-5).

Rey, H.A. *Curious George Rides a Bike.* NY: Houghton, 1952. (George recycles his newspapers into an origami fleet of boats, instructions included, K-2).

Say, Allan, *Tree of Cranes.* New York: Houghton, 1991. (Holiday story, K-3).

Schroeder, Alan. *Lily and the Wooden Bowl:* New York: Delacote Press, 1994. (Japanese folktale, a young girl wears a wooden bowl over her face and overcomes a variety of trials, 3-6).

Topert, Ann. *Grandfather Tang's Story.* New York: Crown Publishers, Inc., 1990. (a tale told with tangrams, K-3).

Tsuchiya, Yukio. *The Faithful Elephants.* Boston: Houghton Mifflin Company, 1988. (a true story about animals, people and war, 3-5).

Math Resources:

Arem, Cynthia. *Conquering Math Anxiety: A Self-Help Workbook.* Pacific Grove, CA: Brooks/Cole Publishing Co., 1993.

Bendick, Jeanne, *Mathematics Illustrated Dictionary: Facts, Figures and People.* New York: Franklin Watts, 1989.

Countryman, J. *Writing to Learn Mathematics: Strategies that Work.* Portsmouth, NH: Heinemann, 1992.

Day, Lucille, Langbort, Carol, Skolnick, Jane. *How to Encourage Girls in Math and Science.* Palo Alto, CA: Dale Seymour Publisher, 1986.

Engel, Peter. Origami: "*The Mathematician's Art,*" Discover. June 1988, pp. 54-61.

Kaplan, Andrew, Keating, Eddie and Boretz, Carrie. *Careers for Number Lovers.* Brookfield, Conn.: Millbrook Press, 1991.

Mathematics Framework for California Public School. Sacramento: California Department of Education, 1992.

National Council of Teachers Mathematics (NCTM), *Professional Standards of Teaching Mathematics.* Reston, VA: Author, 1991.

_____. *Curriculum and Evaluation Standards for School Mathematics.* Reston, VA: Author, 1989.

_____. Olson, Alton T. *Mathematics through Paperfolding.* 1975. (Junior High)

National Research Council. *Everybody Counts: A Report to the Nation on the Future of Mathematics Education.* Washington DC: National Academy Press, 1989.

Paulos, John Allen. *Innumeracy--Mathematical Illiteracy and Its Consequences.* New York: Hill and Wang, 1988.

Phibbs, Mary E. *"Lessons in Listening and Learning,"* The Science Teacher. 58, #7, Oct. 1991, pp. 40-43.

Sinicrope, Rose and Mick, Harold W. *"Multiplication of Fractions through Paper folding,"* Arithmetic Teacher. October 1992, pp. 116-121.

Winter, Stephen S. and Caruso, Joseph. *Spanish Math Terms, Palabras Fundamentales de Mathematicas.* Portland, Maine: J. Weston Walch Publisher, 1993.

Supplies and Other Resources

50 Simple Things Kids Can do to Save the Earth. Andrews and McMeel. The EarthWorks Group, New York: Universal Press Syndicate Company, 1990.

A Whack on the Side of the Head: How You Can be More Creative, Roger von Oech, New York: Warner Books, 1983.

Children's Peace Statue Project. P.O. Box 12888, Albuquerque, New Mexico 847195. ☎ 505-255-1509. Influenced by the children's peace statue in Japan, this one is to be built by American children as a sign of their "Hope for a Peaceful Future." (send $1 and the name of your child, Crane Newsletter and exhibit available).

Earth Savers. Dept. ES2, 1400 16th Street. N.W., Washington, DC 20036. ☎ 800-432-6564. (FREE club program for kids who care about the Earth, includes newsletter, handbook, cards, and activities).

Educators for Social Responsibility. 23 Garden Street, Cambridge, MA 02138. ☎ 617-492-1764. (conflict resolution, environmental awareness, regional meetings).

FASCINATING FOLDS. P.O. Box 2820-235, Torrance, CA 90509-2820. ☎ 800-968-2418. Origami papers and instructional materials. Write for a FREE brochure, sample and Teacher's kit. Send $1.00 for S/H.

Haiku, One Breath Poetry. Naomi Wakan. Canada: Pacific-Rim Publishers, 1993.

The Joyful Child. Dr. Peggy Jenkins. Tucson, Arizona, Harbinger House, 1989.

Teaching Tolerance Magazine. 400 Washington Avenue, Montgomery, AL 36104. ☎ 334-264-0286. (published 2x year, send your request on school letterhead for a FREE subscription).

The Global Link Newsletter. 800 Third Avenue, 37th Floor, New York, New York 10022-7604. ☎ 800-PEACELINE or 800-732-2354. Published by the World Peace Prayer Society, (sponsors Peace Pole Project, Peace Pals and other activities).

Peace & Pole Project. P.O. Box 460097, San Francisco, CA 94146-0097. ☎ 415-641-5085. Peace Poles stand six feet tall and carry the universal message, "May Peace Prevail on Earth" (desk size and other languages available). Promote a fund raiser and purchase a pole to promote world peace.

Women's History Catalog. 7738 Bell Road, Windsor, CA 95492-8518. ☎ 707-838-6000. (See *Outstanding Women in Mathematics and Science*-photo display and more).

✎ WRITE TO US!
Your comments and suggestions are welcome.
Ask a question, share some new ideas,
Send a picture or a story too.
We'll look forward to hearing from you!
Visit our Teachers Corner at FASCINATING FOLDS
WEB SITE: http://www.fascinating-folds.com/paper
MATH IN MOTION ▲ 2417 Vista Hogar ▲ Newport Beach, CA 92660
☎ (714) 721-0633/ 1-800-968-2418/ E-mail: Pearl2@earthlink.net

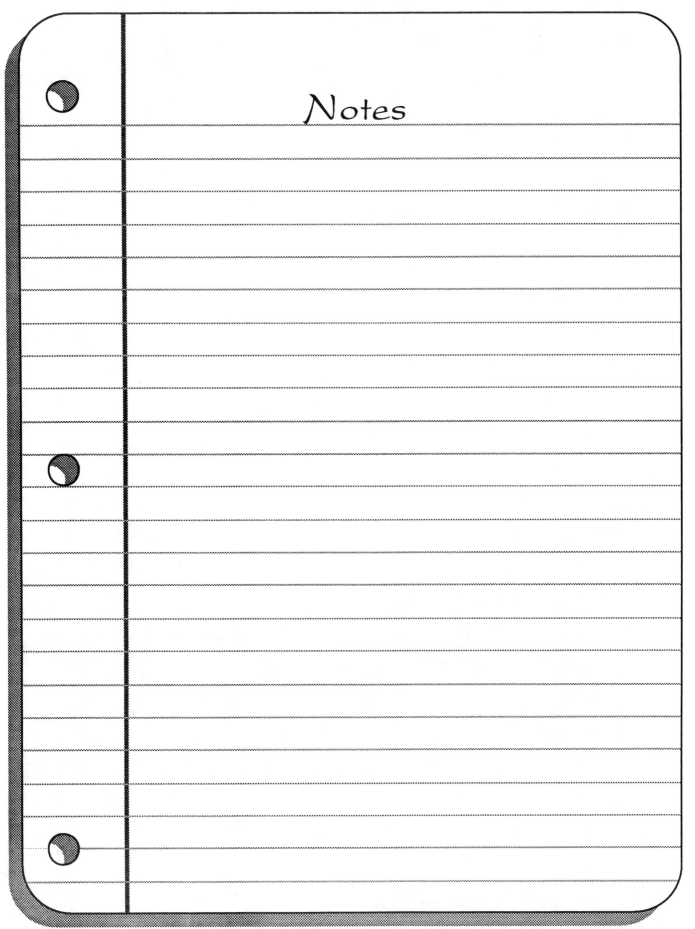

Notes